# Nietzsche

## a biographical introduction

Janko Lavrin

*Charles Scribner's Sons*
*New York*

## Some Other Books by Janko Lavrin

*Aspects of Modernism from Wilde to Pirandello* London 1935
*An Introduction to the Russian Novel* London 1942
*Dostoyevsky* London 1943; New York 1969
*Tolstoy* London 1944; New York 1969
*From Pushkin to Mayakovsky* London 1948
*Pushkin and Russian Literature* London 1947; New York 1969
*Ibsen* London 1950; New York 1969
*Gogol* London 1951; New York 1968
*Goncharov* London 1943; New York 1969
*Lermontov* London 1959
*Russia, Slavdom and the Western World* London 1969
etc.

The original photo used in the front cover design is reproduced by courtesy of the Radio Times Hulton Picture Library, London.

A-1.72 [c]

Printed in the United States of America
Library of Congress Catalog Card Number 79-174651
SBN 684-12671-0 (trade cloth)
SBN 684-12672-9 (trade paper)

# Nietzsche

a biographical introduction

# Contents

Author's note  6

Introduction  7

1 Early striving  11

2 The artifice of self-preservation  31

3 Nietzsche and love  51

4 Anti-religion  62

5 The superman  80

6 The last act  104

7 Nietzsche, Germany and Europe  113

8 A note on Nietzsche and Dostoyevsky  128

9 Conclusion  137

Biographical notes  138

Short bibliography of works in English,
German and French  140

Index  143

## Author's Note

The quotations from Nietzsche's writings are taken from
*The Complete Works of Friedrich Nietzsche*, edited by
Dr Oscar Levy and published by Allen and Unwin. For
the majority of quotations from his letters I am indebted
to Anthony Ludovici's translation *Selected Letters of
Friedrich Nietzsche*, edited by Dr Oscar Levy (Heinemann).
A few passages from his letters and posthumous writings
have been translated by myself. To the publishers and the
translators concerned my thanks and acknowledgments
are due.

All italics shown in the quotations from Nietzsche's
writings follow the original text.

Although based on a previous study of mine this book
contains a considerable amount of new material.

# Introduction

The aim of this book is not only to sum up briefly Friedrich Nietzsche's life and work, but also to state, in as simple terms as possible, what Nietzsche still means, or might mean, to us some seventy years after his death. In the history of modern European thought and culture Nietzsche occupies one of the most provocative and at the same time perplexing positions: provocative, because he challenged all the traditional ideas, beliefs and values of his age; and perplexing, because his work has proved highly stimulating even on account of its inconsistencies and contradictions. His personal fate itself was unusual, and its dramatic character was increased by the fact that after neglect, lasting throughout the whole of his creative life, Nietzsche's work sprang into such vogue that it became, for a while, something of an ideological battle-cry all over Europe. And although his challenge to the whole of our civilization was misinterpreted by his detractors and often even more so by his followers, the passions aroused by his thought set much of the mental and moral climate of our times.

Nietzsche emerged at the dead end of an epoch whose inner and external crises made us witness the gradual bankruptcy of our humanistic traditions. He was one of those who refused to be deluded. While one facet of his thought was visionary and prophetic, the other was intensely critical and full of ominous warnings. As a critic he gave us one of the most merciless diagnoses of our age. As a visionary again he offered to his contemporaries an ideal which in the end proved to be as impossible in practice as it was daring in theory. Unconventional to the uttermost, he fought against any mere theoretical doctrines. What he demanded was a lived and living philosophy – a philosophy which might actively affect our existence. In one of his early essays he jotted down these programmatic words: 'For my part the most important question philosophy has to decide seems to be, how far things have acquired an unalterable stamp and form, and, once the question has been answered, I think it the duty of philosophy to proceed with the task of improving that part of the world which has been recognized as still susceptible of change.' (*Richard Wagner in Bayreuth.*)

Endowed with a strong reforming temperament, Nietzsche was preoccupied above all with those aspects of the world which were 'still susceptible of change' and therefore ought to be changed in the name of what he called an ascending type of man and life. But as he was also an invalid, afflicted by a number of ailments, he had to wage a war on two fronts. One of these was concerned with the improvement of his physical and psychic state of health, while the other touched upon issues which went beyond any personal considerations. The pressure and the strain of this double contest were so great as to end in his mental breakdown, or rather mental death, some ten years before his physical death took place in 1900.

It would be unjust, though, to let Nietzsche's subsequent insanity impair our judgement of the essential character and value of his thought. Compelled to take his own dilemmas seriously indeed, and to 'philosophize with a hammer', as he put it, he fought with an intensity of purpose which made some kind of calamity almost inevitable. The more so because he always tested his thoughts and ideas upon himself regardless of the price he had to pay for such a method. He never hesitated to change his attitudes according to the needs of life rather than those of mere logic. This is why he can be at times as contradictory or even bewildering as life itself. In fact his philosophy often became part and parcel of his life, of his own biography. So much so that the two can hardly be separated at all. Smooth philosophic systems were thus of no use to him. Nor did he bother about them. 'I am not narrow-minded enough for a system,' he wrote, 'not even for my own system.' He concentrated instead on exploring the possibilities of a creative change through life itself.

This was why the well-known Swiss author Karl Spitteler once asserted that six thinkers of Nietzsche's stamp would be of 'more benefit to a nation than myriads of philosophers and savants during a whole century'. It would certainly be futile to deny that Nietzsche, whatever his faults, was not only a great critic, questioner and destroyer, but also one of the great visionaries and myth-makers of our time. His cardinal dilemma was: Can humanity and culture still be saved, or are both doomed to disintegrate and decay beyond repair? The very magnitude of such a question was bound to mobilize in him all the resources available. It also implied a concentration of mind which would wellnigh have surpassed the stamina of an ordinary mortal.

The safest approach to Nietzsche the philosopher is, therefore, through Nietzsche the man. To do this we must however penetrate behind the numerous masks which he used to put on in order to mystify his readers. Does he not himself acknowledge that 'every philosophy also *conceals* a philosophy; every opinion is also a *lurking-place*, every word is also a *mask*'? Blaise Pascal's dictum, 'Se moquer de la philosophie c'est vraiment philosopher', can therefore be safely applied to Nietzsche, though not in the sense used by those voluble popularizers of Nietzsche's philosophy who were only too prone to identify the masks with the man at the risk of missing both.

The first to swear by him were a number of European decadents of the *fin de siècle*. Nietzsche's heroic individualism, preached in an age of threatening uniformity and standardization, must have seemed an alluring relief to them. Prone to confuse his 'beyond good and evil' with their own 'below good and evil', they often pretended to have found in Nietzsche a philosophic sanction for the very profligacy which he so frankly condemned. Other followers of his seized upon his rather complex theory of the 'will to power' in order to justify by it their own tyrannical instincts as something necessary to the growth of life itself. Indeed, many a German imperialist went so far as to proclaim such an outspoken anti-German as Nietzsche a prophet of that aggressive type of nationalism which wrought so much evil during the first half of this century. Even the Luciferean defiance of Nietzsche's struggle against Christianity was mistaken now and then for the 'enlightened' atheism of a penny pamphlet – as if there were not a world of difference between challenging anti-religion and that shallow irreligion which is a result either of indifference or of ignorance, and in most cases of both.

The list could be extended. The philandering Nietzscheans usually remade their idol in their own image, thus turning that tragic martyr of an epoch into a modish figure, or even into a bundle of fashionable slogans. But like so many other fashions the Nietzschean vogue too was followed by a more detached and sober attitude. We are no longer naïve enough to see in Nietzscheanism a panacea for all our ills and troubles. On the other hand, no one can understand the deeper significance of many a crucial dilemma of recent times unless he knows something of Nietzsche's aims and ideas, as well as of his struggle against the age in which he lived. He not only felt the wayward spirit of the age, but also heard the distant rumblings of that volcanic eruption which threatened to destroy our historical heritage and almost succeeded in doing so. Through his diagnosis of our civilization he gave us sufficient warnings what to expect. To all this there should be added his psychological clairvoyance (he is one of the great psychologists of the last century), the sparkling malice of his sarcasms, and the elusive magic of his style in which thought, emotion and intuition collaborate in such a way that each seems to strengthen the other, while at the same time gaining in its own strength thereby. Nor should one forget his biting vivacity which often played such havoc with some of his less discriminating readers. A study of Nietzsche's life and work is still one of those experiences which cannot but cast light upon a number of aspects vital for modern man and the modern age. This alone would be enough to make us indebted to him even when we do not, and cannot, accept him as our infallible guide.

# 1 Early striving

Even a cursory study of Nietzsche is enough to confront one with a number of paradoxes concerning both his personality and his thought. His very birth was something of a paradox, since this most anti-Christian of all modern thinkers came into this world as the son of a pious Lutheran pastor, with at least three generations of respectable and respected divines on his father's and his mother's side. Born in his father's parish of Röcken on 15 October 1844, he was a native of that part of Thüringen whose German population has a strong admixture of Slav blood. Its original inhabitants had been Slavs whom the Germans had first conquered and then assimilated many centuries before. In addition, Nietzsche's family claimed to have been descended from a fugitive Polish count, Nicki (pr. Nietsky). Nietzsche himself felt proud of such an ancestry, and always kept a warm corner in his heart not only for the Poles but for the Slav race in general.*

When the boy was in his fifth year, his father had a heavy fall which proved to be fatal. Nietzsche's widowed mother then moved with her little son and his two years younger sister Elisabeth to the neighbouring town of Naumburg on the river Saale. Here the little Fritz showed himself so outstanding at the local school that at the age of fourteen he was accepted as a pupil by the exclusive Pforta boarding school, where he remained until matriculation. Pforta (or Schulpforta) was a former Cistercian monastery. It had been turned into a purely educational institution during the Reformation and counted among its students a

---

*In one of his last books (*Ecce Homo*) Nietzsche confesses: 'When I think of the number of times in my travels that I have been accosted as a Pole – even by the Poles themselves, and how seldom I have been taken for a German, it seems to me as if I belong to those who have only a sprinkling of German blood in them.'

number of famous names: the romantic poet Novalis, for instance, the philosopher Fichte, the historian Ranke, and the brothers Schlegel. While Nietzsche was a pupil there, Pforta had an excellent staff of teachers. His own interests were divided between poetry, classical studies and also music, for, like his father, he was an excellent musician. Even at that early age he was a good enough pianist to be able to extemporize and even to compose all sorts of melodies – an occupation which he continued in later years. Endowed with a high sense of duty, he was polite and punctilious, but evidently not without occasional lapses. This is what he wrote to his mother in April 1863: 'Last Sunday I got drunk [during an outing] and have no excuse but this, that I did not know how much I could stand and that I happened to be somewhat excited that afternoon. When I returned, Herr Kern, one of the masters, came across me in that condition. He had me called before the Synod on Tuesday, when I was degraded to third of my division and one hour of my Sunday walk was cancelled. You can imagine how depressed and miserable I feel.'

On finishing the Pforta School, Nietzsche entered – in 1864 – the University of Bonn where he intended to study theology and the classics. But neither Bonn nor its University appealed to his taste. As he complained in a letter to his mother (30 June, 1865): 'I am very much disgusted by the bigoted Roman Catholic population here. Often I can scarcely believe that we are in the nineteenth century.' Yet he found in Professor Friedrich Wilhelm Ritschl (1801–76) such an inspiring classical scholar that in the second term he gave up (to his mother's chagrin) theological studies in order to dedicate all his energies to classics, notably to the world and culture of ancient Greece. Among the lasting friends he had made at Bonn was Erwin Rohde, subsequently an authority on ancient Greece. When, in 1865, Professor Ritschl took up an appointment at Leipzig University, both Nietzsche and Rohde followed him there in order to continue their studies under his guidance.

2

Nietzsche's stay at Leipzig, though not eventful, was yet marked by certain incidents which had a decisive effect upon his life. It was quite by chance that one day he acquired an old copy of Schopenhauer's *The World as Will and Idea* (*Die Welt als Wille und Vorstellung*). He read and re-read it continually, as though in a trance, for a fortnight. When he had finished it, his entire world-outlook was changed. This son of a religious country parson instantly embraced Schopenhauer's teaching: that there is no God, no Providence, and no meaning either in life or in the universe. Behind it all there is only the blind will to exist, whatever the pain and suffering implied. This irrational universal Will is the sought for 'thing in itself', the quintessence of all phenomena, and it becomes conscious through man's intellect. And so man alone is aware of the great pain operating through such irrational cosmic force. But he can abate or even suppress it at least in himself through acts of self-denial and resignation which reach their final stage in the oriental Nirvana.

At the University Nietzsche was particularly influenced by pre-Socratic philosophers. Among the early poets who attracted him most was Theognis of Megara whose aristocratic mentality especially appealed to him. He even read a paper on Theognis, which was so good that Professor Ritschl had it published in *Rheinisches Museum* – an exclusive periodical where some of Nietzsche's further contributions also appeared. His studies were interrupted for a while by his military service (in 1867) in an artillery unit at Naumburg, which ended, however, in something resembling a disaster. He described it (on 22 June 1868) in a letter to a former schoolfellow at Pforta, Baron Karl von Gersdorff: 'One day I failed in attempting a smart spring into the saddle, I gave my chest a blow on the pommel and felt a sharp rend in my left side. But I quietly went on riding, and endured the increasing pain for a day and a half. On the evening of the second day, however, I had two fainting fits, and on the third day I lay as if nailed to my bed, suffering the most terrible agony and with a high temperature. . . . From that time onward, for *three whole months*, the suppuration never ceased, and when at last I left my bed, I was naturally so exhausted that I had to learn to walk again.'

Once back in Leipzig, he was introduced, in the autumn of 1868, to Richard Wagner who was paying a visit to his sister Frau Brockhaus – an acquaintance of the Ritschls. It was at Frau Brockhaus's that Nietzsche spent an evening in the company of Wagner, discussing Schopenhauer and music. Wagner seemed to have taken an interest in his young admirer.* At the close of the evening he warmly shook his hand and expressed the hope that they would meet again at some later date.

This second meeting occurred quite soon, owing to Nietzsche's first appointment. His contributions to such a reputable periodical as *Rheinisches Museum* aroused considerable attention among people interested in classical studies. As a result Professor Ritschl received in 1868 an inquiry as to whether his talented pupil would be willing to take on the post of professor of classical philology at Basle University. Ritschl recommended him wholeheartedly, although Nietzsche had not yet taken his Ph.D. At the age of twenty-four he thus became a member of the staff of the oldest university in Switzerland – founded in 1460. When he took on his job, he was fortunate to find among his older colleagues such outstanding scholars as the historian of Greek and Renaissance culture Jacob Burckhardt (1818–97), and the liberal-minded theologian and specialist in Church history Franz Overbeck (1837–1905). Both became his friends and advisers. His post at Basle was also responsible for the renewal of his acquaintance with Wagner.

### 3

Richard Wagner was staying at the time in Tribschen near Lucerne, quite near Basle, and Nietzsche hurried to see

---

* Neitzsche had been previously initiated into Wagner's music by an extract from a piano version of *Tristan and Isolde* which he often played with genuine enthusiasm.

him. He was heartily welcomed by the composer, and also by Cosima Wagner, who had recently left her first husband – the musician and conductor Hans von Buelow. An illegitimate daughter of Franz Liszt, Cosima was nearly thirty years younger than Wagner. She was not conventionally beautiful, but she had a strong personality, and a mind and character of her own. The young visitor from Basle appealed to her on account of his keen intelligence and his equally keen appreciation of Wagner's music. Wagner himself found another bond with Nietzsche in his interest in Schopenhauer and ancient Greece.

Nietzsche's excursions to Tribschen increased in frequency. Eventually he spent most of his week-ends with Wagner and Cosima, and not without profit. On 17 August 1869 he wrote to Erwin Rohde, of Wagner: 'A fruitful, rich and convulsive life, distinctly unconventional and deviating from the average standard of morals. But that is precisely why he stands there firmly rooted in his own power, with his eyes always scanning a distance beyond everything ephemeral, and beyond his age in the finest sense.' And in another letter he refers to Tribschen in these words: 'All that I learn here, and see, and listen to is impossible to explain. Schopenhauer and Goethe, Pindar and Aeschylus are still alive – believe me!' Nietzsche himself was busy at the time with his first major work, a book on Greek tragedy. While gathering material for it he came to hope that a renewal of German spirit at its best might take place through the impact of Hellenism and of Wagner's music as he understood it in those days. He was actually inclined to think he had discovered in Richard Wagner's musical dramas a modern equivalent of such Greek tragedies as those by Aeschylus and Sophocles. This may have been one of the reasons why he decided to call the book *The Birth of Tragedy from the Spirit of Music* (*Die Geburt der Tragoedie aus dem Geiste der Musik*, 1861). But before this piece of research was completed Nietzsche spent another brief period in the German army during the Franco-Prussian War of 1870–1, which further undermined his health. When accepting the post at Basle he had

had to adopt Swiss nationality, yet, full of patriotic zeal, he decided to join the German army as soon as hostilities broke out. Being a Swiss citizen, he was not allowed to fight in the German forces. His bad eyesight was another obstacle. Finally he obtained permission to serve as an ambulance attendant which he did, but with unfortunate results. While conveying some wounded French soldiers in a cattle truck to Karlsruhe, he contracted diphtheria and dysentery, and during his period of convalescence he seems to have revised his former hopes about Germany, and most of all about Prussia. On 7 November 1870 he wrote to his friend Gersdorff: 'Between ourselves, I regard the Prussia of today as a power full of the greatest dangers for culture. . . . We must be philosophical enough to keep our presence of mind in the midst of all this intoxication, so that no thief may come to rob or steal from us – what the greatest military feats or the highest national exaltation never replace. . . . Much fighting will be necessary for the coming period of culture, and for this work we must keep ourselves in readiness.' And only five weeks later he wrote to his mother and sister: 'I am gradually losing all my sympathy for Germany's present war of conquest.'

Much of Nietzsche's convalescence after the infection was spent at Naumburg where he was looked after by his mother and sister, In February 1871 he left – together with his sister Elisabeth – for Lugano in the hope of finding there some treatment for insomnia and migraine. While crossing the St Gotthard Pass, he found himself talking to a rather distinguished-looking old man who turned out to be the famous patriot and fighter for Italian freedom, Mazzini – a chance meeting which remained vivid in Nietzsche's memory.

4

On his return to Basle Nietzsche's health was extremely precarious, but he continued to work upon his *Birth of Tragedy* which came out on the last day of 1871. The book however, was too full of startling new ideas to be widely appreciated and comparatively few copies were sold.

Wagner and Cosima were, of course, enchanted by it. 'I have never read a more beautiful book than yours', Wagner wrote to Nietzsche. 'Everything in it is magnificent. . . . I said to Cosima: "After you it is he whom I love most."' Rohde and Overbeck were also appreciative, but Professor Ritschl was diplomatically silent. And not without reason, since Nietzsche here disregarded the old conventional views about Greece, starting from the commonplace that ancient Greeks were a harmonious, optimistic and cheerful people. On the contrary, he put forward the argument that they (in this case the Greeks of the sixth century BC) had suffered from incredible pessimism and distrust of life. They were, moreover, ravaged by rivalries, jealousies and intrigue – a view which coincided with Burckhardt's attitude. But he did not stop there: in his conception of Greek tragedy as represented by Aeschylus, for example, he saw an attempt to overcome their pessimistic attitude which rejects life, by that tragic attitude which is beyond pessimism and optimism, and bravely affirms life in spite of its pain and evil.

In his preface to a later edition of this work (with the new subtitle of *Hellenism and Pessimism*) Nietzsche amplified his idea by the following passage: 'Is pessimism *necessarily* the sign of decline, of decay, of failure, of exhausted and weakened instincts – as was the case with the Indians, as is to all appearance the case with us "modern men" and Europeans? Is there a pessimism of *strength*? An intellectual predilection for what is hard, awful, evil, problematic in existence, owing to well-being, to exuberant health, to fullness of existence? . . . What means tragic myth to the Greeks of the best, strongest, bravest era? And the prodigious phenomenon of the Dionysian? And that which was born thereof, tragedy? And that of which tragedy died – the Socratism of morality, the dialectics, contentedness and cheerfulness of the theoretical man? – indeed, might not this very Socratism be a sign of decline, of weariness, of disease, of anarchically disintegrating instincts?'

In the same book he laid particular stress upon the

distinction between the Dionysian and the Apollonian elements in the Greek consciousness. (Both labels have since been largely accepted in Nietzsche's interpretation.) In the Dionysian phenomenon he saw the orgiastic and ecstatic affirmation of that primordial unity between man and Nature which preceded and often even precluded any process of individuation. When all barriers were thus broken down in a state of animal intoxication, the human self was in danger of disappearing, or rather disintegrating, in the chaos of the amorphous pre-individual oneness; but it was saved by the intervention of the opposite Apollonian element of harmony, form, measure and individuation. A dynamic balance between Dionysus and Apollo, between the Dionysian and Apollonian impulses, was responsible – according to Nietzsche – for all that was best in Greek art and culture. It also saved the Greeks from sinking into their own pessimism, for which their tragic art provided the collective outlet.

While proclaiming that 'art is the highest task and the properly metaphysical activity of this life', Nietzsche stresses here the fact that it is only as an aesthetic phenomenon that the existence of man and the world appears justified. At the same time he develops the argument that Attic tragedy as art was equally Dionysian and Apollonian. The Dionysian part was expressed by the chorus and its music, whereas the Apollonian vision or dream-world was shown on the stage. And the power of music, while reaching its highest satisfaction in tragedy, was also able to invest the myths with a new and profound significance.

Nietzsche's attack upon the purely intellectual and theorizing 'Socratic' mentality (which, according to him, caused the decline of Greek tragedy after Aeschylus and Sophocles) was followed by an equally scathing onslaught upon modern opera, but with the reservation that 'out of the Dionysian root of the German spirit' a power has arisen which is hostile to Socratic culture. This new power is German music from Bach to Beethoven and Wagner. A return to the spirit of tragedy is thus possible through the German spirit itself, provided the latter is willing to 'learn implicitly of one people – the Greeks, of whom to learn at all is a high honour and a rare distinction'. For in some 'inaccessible abyss' the German spirit has still preserved its Dionysian strength, both in its music and its tragic myths. The implication was, of course, that Wagner was the bearer of this kind of music. According to Schopenhauer, of all the arts music alone is a direct expression of the 'will to exist' and conveys its deepest mysteries. Wagner's works were regarded by the Nietzsche of that period as an up-to-date Teutonic equivalent of ancient Greek tragedy before Euripides. He saw in Wagner not only a man who was larger than life but also a genius able to express the German tragic myths through a new variety of 'Dionysian' music.

Wagner himself was highly gratified by such a view. The more so because at that very time he had left Tribschen and settled at Bayreuth in Bavaria, where he was anxious to establish a theatre of his own. This theatre was to be a kind of temple designed to produce only his works – a plan in which he was soon to succeed.

5

On 22nd May 1872, Richard Wagner laid the first stone for the theatre. Among the numerous guests gathered there for the occasion was the elderly authoress and champion of radical opinions, Malwida von Meysenbug, who met Nietzsche for the first time and remained his loyal (if somewhat motherly) friend even during the worst trials of his life, although she hardly accepted or even understood much of his philosophy.* At Bayreuth,

* Malwida von Meysenbug (pr. Maisenboog) – 1816–1903 – made a mark with her interesting autobiography, *The Memoirs of an Idealist* (*Memoiren einer Idealistin*), published in three volumes in 1876. Although of aristocratic birth, she became an ardent revolutionary in 1848, but when the reaction took the upper hand in Germany she had to flee abroad. She was keen on emancipation of women, yet not at the expense of their femininity. As a fugitive rebel she had lived for years in London where she taught Alexander Herzen's children. After Herzen's death she adopted his daughter Olga.

however, the celebrated composer was no longer the
Wagner Nietzsche had known at Tribschen. Conscious
of his own greatness, he had become haughty, intolerant
and jealous. Nietzsche, on the other hand, was in a restive
mood. After the failure of his book* he must have had
some further misgivings about the condition and the
possibilities of German culture. He was also on the look-
out for opportunities to say what he thought without
beating about the bush. Aggressiveness became one of
his needs and tonics.

A pretext for it was provided by one of the celebrated
though superficial 'best-sellers' of the period, *The Old and
the New Faith (Der alte und der neue Glaube)* by David
Friedrich Strauss. Its author discussed in it rather
complacently the new 'scientific' outlook which according
to him was destined not only to replace the obsolete old
religions, but also to provide a solution for man's burning
problems of existence and save him from vexation of spirit.
The book became a kind of banner in the so-called
*Kulturkampf* (cultural struggle) between the liberal and the
conservative intellectuals throughout Germany. It was
this work and its author that Nietzsche now attacked in his
long essay, *David Strauss, the Confessor and Writer (D.S.,
der Bekenner und Schriftsteller,* 1873). He pointed out in
unmistakable terms the shallowness of the author's
attitude; at the same time he launched a virulent campaign
against such Culture-Philistines (*Kulterphilister*) as Strauss
himself. Strongly preoccupied with cultural values,
Nietzsche warned the Germans not to swell and swagger
because of their recent victories over the French. Their
military triumph was in fact only too likely to be accompanied by a cultural defeat, signs of which were already
visible in the prestige enjoyed by Philistines of the D. F.
Strauss brand. Even in the celebrated German erudition,
with its cult of quantitative knowledge, Nietzsche saw an
encumbrance and a danger to creative culture. To repeat

* His schoolfellow from Pforta, Professor Ulrich von
Moellendorff (1848–1931), wrote of *The Birth of Tragedy* as a
'nest of imbecilities'.

his own words, 'Culture, is, before all things, the unity of
artistic style, in every expression of the life of the people.
Abundant knowledge and learning, however, are not
essential to it, nor are they a sign of its existence; and at a
pinch, they might coexist much more harmoniously with
the very opposite of culture – with barbarity: that is to say,
with a complete lack of style, or with a riotous jumble of
styles.' He concludes that 'the mind of a cultured Philistine
must have become very unhinged; for precisely what culture repudiates he regards as culture itself'. An unpatriotic essay of this kind was bound to provoke some violent
criticisms, and it did. 'All the powers are mobilized against
me,' Nietzsche complained to Gersdorff apropos an article
in the *Grenzbote* (27 October 1873). 'It is emphatically
declared that I shall be ostracized from every German
university and that Basle will probably do likewise.'

In July 1875 the rehearsals of Wagner's Nibelungen
tetralogy – *Rheingold, Walkyrie, Siegfried, The Twilight
of the Gods* – were taking place at Bayreuth. Nietzsche
received an invitation but did not accept it, partly because
his health had taken a turn for the worse, and partly
because of his growing disappointment in Wagner. He
visited Bayreuth, however, in the following summer,
when the operas were being presented with unprecedented
success. Yet the relationship between Nietzsche and
Wagner was now entirely different from that of the good
old Tribschen days. Wagner triumphant was, in spite of
his genius, not a pleasant sight to behold. Bumptious,
grandiloquent (like the accomplished actor that he was)
and spoiled by adulation, he evidently expected further
eulogies from Nietzsche almost as a matter of course. Yet
in his incurable opportunism he was already philandering
with such mystical or pseudo-mystical Christian themes as
his *Parsifal* – calculated to impress Germany and Europe.

Dissatisfied with it all, Nietzsche decided to break with
Wagner. Nevertheless, in the same year he wrote his
*Richard Wagner in Bayreuth* which was a kind of gallant
farewell to his old-time friend, for he praised in this essay
what he once had regarded in Wagner as worthy of praise.

In his previous essay *Schopenhauer as Educator* (1874) one feels, behind all his admiration for the great philosopher, that Nietzsche already nourished a certain opposition to Schopenhauer's cult of Nirvana and resignation: even if the universe be blind and entirely meaningless, a strong individual can still say 'Yes' to life and affirm it through his will to create and breed a higher type of man, for the sake of a higher type of life. All that helps this aim is good, all that obstructs and impedes it is evil. A similar attitude was expressed in Nietzsche's essay *The Use and Abuse of History* in which he clearly stated that the 'aim of mankind can ultimately be in its highest examples'.

If during his first period the young Nietzsche was still in danger of regarding a romantic-aesthetic escape from both life and action as something desirable, he now challenged such a temptation as soon as he realized that for an invalid like himself this would be the line of least resistance, and therefore a proof of weakness. So in the second period of his activities he discarded such illusions, especially those provided by Schopenhauer's philosophy and Wagner's music. Years later (in 1888) he acknowledged, in his *Nietzsche contra Wagner,* that every act and every philosophy 'may be regarded either as a cure or as a stimulant to ascending or declining life: they always presuppose suffering and sufferers. But there are two kinds of sufferers: those that suffer from overflowing vitality, who need Dionysian art and require a tragic insight into, and a tragic outlook upon, the phenomenon of life; – and there are those who suffer from *reduced* vitality, and who crave for repose, quietness, calm seas, or else the intoxication, the spasm, the bewilderment which art and philosophy provide. Revenge upon life itself – this is the most vuluptuous form of intoxication for such indigent souls! ... Now Wagner responds quite as well as Schopenhauer to the twofold cravings of these people – they both deny life, they both slander it but precisely on this account they are my antipodes.'

It was during the years of his mounting suffering that Nietzsche was determined to say 'Yes' to life in spite of all.

This was why he turned away from Wagner and Schopenhauer, however important the part both of them had played in his early manhood.

6

The four essays mentioned were published together in Nietzsche's *Thoughts out of Season* (*Unzeitgemaesse Betrachtungen*). Its two volumes appeared in 1876 and concluded the first period of his activities. The main feature of this period was his romantic appreciation of art as a 'metaphysical comfort', while his leaning upon Schopenhauer, Wagner, and the pre-Socratic Greeks was helping him to work out his own outlook upon life. The phase which followed was, however, not only a revision of his first period, but also a reaction against it. From this time Nietzsche freed himself from Schopenhauer and Wagner, as well as any romantic metaphysics. What mattered to him now was a positivist scientific outlook, sharp analysis, and a merciless onslaught on all aspects of decadence, whether individual or social. This involved a virulent criticism of his epoch, beginning with the two volumes of his *Human-all too-Human* (*Menschliches Allzumensch-liches*, 1878), written in terse aphorisms – a method Nietzsche had to adopt on account of his bad eyesight which often prevented him from any prolonged reading and writing.

As for outward stimuli, he found them this time in such masters of irony as Montaigne, Voltaire, Chamfort and La Rochefoucauld. What he admired in them was their keen realistic sense, coupled with a witty and smiling intelligence and that lightness of touch which knew how to play even with depth and be 'superficial from profundity'. The playful ease of the French *esprit* was certainly remote from that *Geist der Schwere* (the spirit of gravity) which Nietzsche regarded as a kind of blight upon the German mind and character. No wonder he also learned from the French (including Pascal) the pregnant and laconic form of expression which stood him in good stead in his own aphorisms. Of the later Frenchmen he disliked Flaubert and Zola, but was enthusiastic about Stendhal who, he thought, was one of the most subtle psychologists of the age. There were other foreign influences, from Emerson to Dostoyevsky; but whatever Nietzsche took from them, he transmuted in such a way as to make it his own.

The same could be said of the impact of those Germans whose works and personalities he admired. They belonged to an earlier Germany – the Germany of Goethe, Schiller and Hölderlin – whose humanistic culture had not yet been crushed by the weight of militarism and imperialism. Nietzsche was alive to the fascination of Goethe's genius, especially to that overflowing yet well balanced and vital mind so steeped in Europe as a whole that it was devoid of any nationalistic parochialism. Schiller may have been occasionally jeered at (on account of his moralizing rhetorics) by Nietzsche; on the other hand, he could not but admire Schiller's fighting spirit, full of a militant faith in the power of art and of true cultural values. With the great poet Friedrich Hölderlin (1770–1843) Nietzsche above all shared his love for ancient Greece, however different his own idea of Greece and the ancient Greek mentality may have been from that of Hölderlin.*

At the time of writing his *Human-all-too-Human* Nietzsche was working towards intellectual freedom in the French sense. He even called this work 'a book for free spirits', and dedicated it to Voltaire. What he meant by it he explained in a passage ending in this succinct formula: 'You should have power over your pro and contra, and learn how to put them forth and withdraw them again in accordance with your higher purpose.' The 'purpose' he had in mind was the breeding of a superior type of man – an aim which gave a kind of unity to his endeavours and which, from now on, took an increasingly strong emphasis in his writings. It was also accompanied by a relentless fight against the decay of his own diseased body. No wonder that in this struggle he found a promising ally in

* Nietzsche, who was also a poet of no mean quality, was partly influenced by Hölderlin's dithyrambic verse, which he manipulated with great skill.

modern biology which he adapted, or did his best to adapt, to his vision of a new man and mankind.

As early as April 1873 (which was one of his more pessimistic periods) he wrote to Malwida von Meysenbug that the world was 'now waiting for the man of *deeds*, who strips off the habit of centuries and sets a better example for posterity to follow'. By the man of deeds he understood the exceptional individual who is strong enough to take upon himself the heaviest tasks in order to improve and ennoble human existence as a whole. It was in this spirit that he had addressed his audience in his essay *The Use and Abuse of History* (*Vom Nutzen und Nachtheil der Historie*) a blend of his own hero-worship and of Schopenhauer's cult of genius, in the solemn language of his first period: 'One giant calls to the other across the waste spaces of time, and the high spirit-talk goes on undisturbed by the wanton noisy dwarfs who creep among them. The task of history is to be a mediator between these, and even to give the motive help and power to produce the great man.'

### 7

His own tendency towards the ennobling (*Veredlung*) of life and man was fostered above all by two factors: a reaction against the Philistine vulgarity and meanness of the age, and his faith in the possibility of rearing a higher type of human species whatever the difficulties. With his aristocratic fastidiousness he was and remained a virtuoso in contempt for a commercialized age in which everything was debased to its lowest level. What he thought of the vulgarization and plebeianization of life all the world over he stated, with his usual emphasis, in his writings, and in certain passages of his principal work, *Thus Spake Zarathustra* (*Also Sprach Zarathustra*, begun in 1882), where he summed up his attitude in passages such as the following:

'I asked once, and I almost suffocated with my question: What! Is the rabble also necessary for life? Are poisoned fountains necessary, and stinking fires, and filthy dreams, and maggots in the bread of life?

'Not my hatred, but my loathing gnawed hungrily at my life! Oh, oft-times I became weary of spirit, when I found even the rabble spiritual!

'And on the rulers I turned my back, when I saw what they now called ruling, the traffic and bargain for power – with the rabble!

'Amongst people of strange language did I dwell, with stopped ears, so that the language of their trafficking might remain strange unto me, and their bargaining for power.

'And holding my nose, I went morosely through all the yesterdays and todays of the scribbling rabble!

'Like a cripple become deaf, and blind, and dumb – thus have I lived long; that I might not live with the power-rabble, the scribble-rabble and the pleasure-rabble.

'What has happened to me? How have I freed myself from loathing? Who has rejuvenated mine eye? How have I flown to the height where no rabble any longer sits at the wells?

'Did my loathing itself create for me wings and fountain-divining powers? Verily, to the loftiest heights had I to fly, to find again the well of delight! And there is a life at whose waters none of the rabble drinks with me.'

Unable to withstand the world as it was, Nietzsche *had* to create, by contrast, an imaginary world of his own 'before which one could bow the knee' without blushing. The uprooted romantic in him thus made an effort to triumph not only over his scorn but even over his doubts; the more so because he never lost the innate zest of a born educator and reformer. Urges of this kind were enough to deflect his philosophy from Schopenhauer's pessimistic resignation to his own dynamic will to power, which was destined to play such a conspicuous part in his teaching and to re-echo (in its grotesquely distorted aspects) even in modern politics. At the same time he never lost his enthusiasm for the ancient Greeks, notably for those of the sixth century BC, among whom, it seemed to him, the conditions were exceptionally conducive to rearing superior individuals. This was why in his unfinished essay,

*We Philologists* (*Wir Philologen,* 1874), he confessed he was interested 'only in the relations of a people to the rearing of individual men, and among the Greeks the conditions were unusually favourable for the development of the individual. *With the help of favourable means great individuals might be reared who would be both different from and higher than those who heretofore have owed their existence to mere chance. Here we may still be hopeful.'*

Such a blend of ancient Greece, of eugenics and modified Darwinism on the part of Nietzsche was less strange than it looked. In spite of his own deprecation of Darwin, Nietzsche yet accepted certain tenets of Darwinism. The principle of the 'survival of the fittest' actually became – under the new label of the 'will to power' – one of the cornerstones of his sociology. The survival of the strong exceptional individual was however interpreted by him as a continuous effort for the maintenance and the increase of one's power in the struggle for the quality of existence. Hence Nietzsche was driven to regard the figure of the idealized warrior as being eminently suitable for the *élite* of which he dreamed. And since he waged a simultaneous war with himself, he naturally advocated hardness and spartan ruthlessness for both battles.

8

It was during this second period (after 1876) that Nietzsche's eyesight, as well as his general condition, deteriorated to such an extent as often to make it difficult for him to write down even the notes and fragments for his further works. Sometimes he had to dictate them to the young composer Peter Gast, whose real name was Heinrich Koeselitz and who at the time was a student at Basle University. Another helpful friend was Dr Paul Rée, a talented young philosopher of Jewish extraction, an admirer of Schopenhauer, a good conversationalist and stimulating companion. A considerable amount of comfort came also from Nietzsche's sister Elisabeth who, in contrast to her brother, was always sure of herself, practical, provincially prim and inclined to be rather petty in her conventional outlook upon life. Yet whatever the differences between the two, she adored her brother and did all she could to make his life easier. Unfortunately Nietzsche's ailments (migraine, stomach troubles, sleeplessness, etc.) became so painful at times that in 1879 he resigned his professorship at Basle. From now on he became an 'eternal fugitive' (as he called himself), looking in all sorts of places and climates for at least some improvement in his steadily deteriorating health.

Having been granted a small pension by the university, he turned into a restless expatriate, living now in Switzerland, then in Italy or on the French Riviera, with occasional visits to Germany. During the short periods of release from physical pain he worked with feverish energy in order to say what he wanted. Yet separated from most of his old friends, he felt increasingly lonely. His isolation became the more painful because the books he published after *The Birth of Tragedy* found neither readers nor reviewers. They were either attacked or else ignored. This applied not only to *Human-all-too-Human*, but to such excellent products of his second period as *The Dawn of Day* (*Die Morgenröthe*, 1881) and *The Joyful Wisdom* (*Die fröhliche Wissenschaft*, 1882). Feeling utterly 'out of season' in his age, he was also treated as such.

Nietzsche spent most of winter and spring 1880–1 in Genoa. It was here that he wrote his book of aphorisms *The Dawn of Day*. The title itself had a double meaning, referring on the one hand to a temporary improvement of his physical condition,* and on the other to his freedom from any 'romantic' influences. In the summer of the same year he went to the village of Sils Maria in upper Engadine. Here he occupied a tiny private room and took his meals in the local inn, close by the church. He spent most of the time walking in the surroundings and enjoying the mountain air at least as long as the sunny weeks lasted. It was at this time that he first formulated his idea of 'eternal recurrence' ('die ewige Wiederkunft'). The gist of it can be stated in a few words. Since in the blind eternal

* But see Nietzsche's own reference to his condition, page 32.

world-process the atoms are continually changing their positions, the universe must pass, during countless aeons, through all the combinations possible and return again and again to the states it had been in before. This means that the very same conditions in which it is at present will repeatedly recur with exactly the same people, the same moments of life and history.

The idea itself was not new. It could have been traced at least as far back as the Greek Pythagoreans, to Zeno's stoicism, and further still to Hindu cosmogony. Still, its impact upon Nietzsche was tremendous. It meant nothing less than a substitute for eternity in a materialist world devoid of any scope or meaning. Nietzsche felt a kind of exultation at this discovery made '6000 feet above the sea and much higher above all human things'. It also inspired him with the vision of a prophet announcing such an idea to the world – an early flash of his *Thus Spake Zarathustra* which was soon to introduce the third (and last) phase of his creative activities.

9

After a not very pleasant sea-journey to Sicily Nietzsche stayed in the early weeks of 1882 at Messina. It was here that he received an invitation from Malwida to come and spend the spring in Rome in the company of his friend Dr Rée who at that time was in the grip of a serious emotional upset caused by a fascinating Russian girl-student Lou Salomé, one of Malwida's friends who was staying at the time with her mother in Rome. The daughter of a distinguished Russian general of distant French (Huguenot) origin, Lou belonged to the social élite of St Petersburg but was already at that early age independent and stubborn enough to have decided, despite her mother's objections (her father died in 1879), to study abroad and live a life of her own. While in Rome she frequently came to see Malwida at her flat in via Pulveriera and there she met the sympathetic philosopher Dr Rée, whose pessimistic outlook must have intrigued her. During their long discussions and night walks in the streets of Rome, Rée became so carried away by his alert Russian companion that before long he made a proposal of marriage to her. But Lou, friendly though her feelings towards him were, was not in the least interested in marriage.

In the deep fits of depression which followed, Dr Rée often mentioned the name of his friend Nietzsche and, since Lou expressed a wish to see him, he was duly invited to come to Rome where he was to meet *die interessante Russin*. Without much delay Nietzsche left Messina for Rome where he was introduced to Lou by Rée himself in, of all places, St Peter's. As might have been expected, Nietzsche too fell in love with her almost at the first encounter. The talks they had together convinced him that she was 'well prepared for any kind of problem' in which he himself was engrossed at the time. Full of admiration for such an unexpected companion, he too began to think of marrying her. But Lou, who was intellectually very precocious, seemed to be emotionally retarded to the extent of accepting men's friendship without any sexual *arrière-pensées* or matrimonial designs. What she appreciated instead was mental stimulation and excitement. Lou's father (whom she adored) had died when she was seventeen and she evidently suffered from a 'father complex' for years afterwards. As a young girl she was also under the strong intellectual influence of a man who was more than twice her age, Hendrik Gillot, pastor of the Dutch Evangelical Church at St Petersburg. Fascinated by her, Gillot himself wanted to marry her, but she would not hear of any emotional entanglement, least of all marriage.

When Nietzsche proposed to her (not personally but – strangely enough – through his friend and rival Dr Rée) she refused. Still, Nietzsche would not take no for an answer. After weeks of hopes and of emotional complications, it came to a climax in the summer of the same year.

But before dealing with this episode which had a considerable impact upon his life and work, it might be expedient to probe the nature of that illness with which he waged constant war, and to which he finally succumbed.

# 2 The artifice of self-preservation

I

The real cause of the malady which eventually drove Nietzsche to insanity still remains somewhat obscure. His father, Karl Ludwig Nietzsche, died in 1848 of inflammation of the brain, but this was supposed to be due to an accident which occurred when his son was nearly five years old. Dr Gaston Vorberg, in his book *Nietzsche's Illness and Collapse* (*Ueber Nietzsches Krankheit und Zusammenbruch*, 1933) attributes both Nietzsche's illness and final catastrophe to syphilis. Among the records of the Jena Clinic, where Nietzsche stayed for a while as a patient in 1889, the following entry can be read: '1866. *Syphilitische Ansteckung*' (*syphilitic infection*).*

If this diagnosis is correct, then quite a few aspects of Nietzsche's case become clearer. In his day syphilis was considered incurable, or almost incurable, since its usual consequence was physical and mental breakdown. This alone would have been enough to make such a sufferer as Nietzsche mobilize his power of resistance on a scale as formidable as was the illness itself. His struggle for health would then certainly have amounted to a duel with fate. Yet whatever the origin of Nietzsche's disease is held to be, even during his first years at Basle the young professor suffered terribly from nervous complaints, headaches and a gradual weakening of his eyesight. The attacks increased so alarmingly that in 1879 he had to resign his post, after which he wandered over a large area of Europe in search of places that might bring him some relief.

'I have resigned my professorship and am going to the mountains,' he wrote to his publisher in May 1879. 'I am

---

* A careful examination of this problem can be found in E. P. Podach's *The Madness of Nietzsche* (*Nietzsches Zusammenbruch*, 1930). Nor is it without interest that in his novel *Doctor Faustus*, Thomas Mann has made use of Nietzsche's case for his main hero – a musician of genius who, in the end, also goes mad as a result of a similar infection.

on the verge of despair, and there is hardly any hope left. My sufferings have been too great, too persistent.' He signed his letter 'A half-blind man'. In the same year he wrote to Peter Gast: 'Now I am in the middle of my life and so "encircled by death" that it may be here any minute. Judging by the nature of my suffering I must count upon a *sudden* death through convulsions.' 'I am on the verge of despair,' he complained (in Latin) to Professor Overbeck two years later. 'Suffering is crushing my life and my will. Oh, what months, what a summer have I gone through! I experienced as many physical torments as there were changes in the sky. Five times I invoked Death as my only physician. I hoped that yesterday would be my last day – hoped in vain.' And in a letter to Baron von Seydlitz (as late as February 1888): 'It was not "proud silence" that kept my lips sealed to everyone all this time, but rather the humble silence of a sufferer who was ashamed of giving away the extent of his own pain. When an animal is ill it crawls into its cave – so does *la bête philosophe*. It is so seldom that a friendly voice comes my way. I am alone, absurdly alone, and in my relentless subterranean war against all that mankind has honoured and loved hitherto, I myself seem unwittingly to have become something of a cave, something concealed that can no longer be found even when it is a definite object of one's reach.'

The last letter with its 'cave' and 'subterranean war against all that mankind has hitherto honoured and loved', calls to mind Dostoyevsky's cruel *Notes from the Underworld* (*Zapiski iz podpolya*), a French translation of which, under the title of *L'esprit souterrain*, Nietzsche had recommended only a few months earlier in a letter to Overbeck. Yet isolated and suffering as he was, he believed he could ward off a collapse by mental and psychic means, that is, by fighting for such a great task as would make him forget or else defy everything there was to defy, and most of all his own illness. This produced an inner tension strong enough to mobilize in sheer self-defence all his vitality so long as it lasted. And to make it last longer, he was also practically compelled to lay more and more stress on that factor of physical fitness which formed so large a part of his philosophy, from his second stage on. Since Nietzsche's own life had to be defended, he turned his philosophy all the more readily into a defence of life as a whole. His quest for philosophic truths thus became increasingly also a quest for health, accompanied by his ceaseless wanderings, valuations and transvaluations. His outward existence after Basle was reduced to a futile and monotonous rushing from place to place in order to improve his health. His inner life, on the other hand, grew in intensity for the very reason that he had to make use of all his mental and moral resources in order to increase his physical resistance itself. This was how he transformed his philosophy into an essential part of his own biography.

2

Readers of Nietzsche are familiar with the passages in which the invalid thinker propounds – quite in the spirit of Kant – the futility of all endeavours to grasp the essence of things ('das Ding an sich'), since we find in them only what we ourselves have put into them. Or, as he contends, it is the habits of our senses that have 'wrapped us up in the tissue of living sensations which in their turn crouch at the base of all judgements and "knowledge" – and there are no means of exit or escape to the real world! We are like spiders in our webs, and whatever we may catch in them it will only be something that our web is capable of catching.'* On this premise alone, to say nothing of the pressing personal reasons, Nietzsche would have felt inclined to abandon the old-fashioned abstract quest and replace it by something tangible. If the search for transcendental truths leads nowhere, then our duty is to direct our efforts towards what is more definite and concrete, that is towards the defence as well as affirmation of life itself, with man's individual fate in the centre.

Once such a position has been adopted, one is likely to regard as important those factors which foster a vigorous

* *The Dawn of Day.*

life. The principal thing is no longer to chase the inaccessible 'truth', but to impose upon the chaos of life as much sense and regularity as is required by our earthly biological existence at its best. And since from a metaphysical standpoint a proceeding of this kind involves the risk of indulging in errors, we can at least draw a line between the life-bringing and the life-destroying errors. In Nietzsche's words: '*Truth is that kind of error* without which a certain species cannot exist. The value for life is ultimately decisive.' (*The Joyful Wisdom.*)

The distinction between true and false in the old metaphysical sense is thus eliminated, or at least ignored. It all amounts to the question as to 'how far an opinion is life-furthering, life-preserving, species-rearing'. Nietzsche even maintains that the falsest opinions are often most indispensable in this respect, since without a recognition of fictions, without a constant counterfeiting of the world man could not live. '*To recognize untruth as the condition of life,* that is certainly to impugn the traditional ideas of value in a dangerous manner, and a philosophy which ventures to do so is thereby alone placed beyond good and evil.' And again: 'According to my way of thinking, "truth" does not necessarily mean the opposite of error, but in the most fundamental cases merely the relation of different errors to each other. Thus one error might be older, deeper than another, perhaps altogether ineradicable, one without which organic creatures like ourselves could not exist.' In another aphorism Nietzsche goes so far as to contend that behind the 'will to truth' in the old metaphysical sense, there might even be 'a disguised will to death' ('ein verstecker Wille zum Tode').

In this 'pragmatic' defence of 'life' in its physiological and earthly sense Nietzsche waged a war on behalf of his own personal life that was at stake all the time. And he did his best to make his philosophy as effective a strategic tool as possible in both self-defence and attack. But in order to do this with a clear conscience he had to expose or debunk the official 'objective' philosophy as a comedy of self-

interest; to show in fact that there was no such thing as a
disinterested search after truth for its own sake. Suspecting
personal reasons – conscious or unconscious – behind it all,
Nietzsche made the refutation of any cocksure transcendental truth a prerequisite of truthfulness itself. Hence
his contempt for canonized philosophies and philosophers,
beginning with Kant. 'The spectacle of the Tartuffery of
old Kant, equally stiff and decent, with which he entices
us into the dialectic by-ways that lead (more correctly,
mislead) to his categorical "imperative" – makes us
fastidious ones smile, and we find no small amusement in
spying out the subtle tricks of old moralists and ethical
preachers. Or, still more so, the hocus-pocus in mathe-
matical form by means of which Spinoza has clad his
philosophy in mail and mask – in fact, the "love of *his*
wisdom", to translate the term fairly and squarely – in
order thereby to strike terror at once into the heart of the
assailant who should dare to cast a glance at that invincible
maiden, that Pallas Athene; how much personal timidity
and vulnerability does this masquerade of a sickly recluse
betray?' (*Beyond Good and Evil.*)

Such were the tenets of Nietzsche's thought and quest
after he had overcome his admiration of Schopenhauer
and Wagner. What mattered to him now more than
anything else was life in its ascending aspects, whereas in
the work of his two former idols he saw only a decadent
flight from life.

### 3

Nietzsche thus largely reduced philosophy to a weapon,
and a sophisticated one at times, in his fight for self-
preservation. Here, at any rate, his strategy became
thoroughly Machiavellian. He adopted or else discarded
certain views and ideas according to the needs of his own
physique and – frank as he was – made no secret of this.
'The snake that cannot cast his skin perishes. So it is too
with those minds which are prevented from changing their
views: they cease to be minds.' Suspicious of all firm
convictions as such, Nietzsche was ready to cast his skin

whenever an operation of this kind was vitally necessary. As a result his work does not resemble a philosophy in the traditional sense – it is rather a process of spontaneous ideas flowing in brilliant if somewhat bewildering outbursts. The phases of this process may have differed, yet his inconsistencies and contradictions were united to a large extent in the physiological principle which underlies the whole of Nietzsche's strategy, so aptly styled by him as 'the artifice of self-preservation'.

The first phase of his thought, during which he was under the influence of Schopenhauer, reveals him as full of the preoccupations characteristic of an ambitious but still somewhat old-fashioned reformer and educator of men. He saw the ideal of humanity in the philosopher, the tragic artist and the saint. But during his second, 'positivist' and scientific, period his desire to produce a higher – physiologically higher – type of man became paramount. Finally, in his third period this very type culminated in his aesthetic-romantic ideal of the superman as devised and represented by his myth of Zarathustra.

These three phases abound in contradictions, but Nietzsche perpetrated them honestly, without any reticence. They were an essential part of his 'artifice of self-preservation' at a time when any preconceived dogmatic convictions might have hampered that freedom of strategy which was demanded by his will to health. What mattered to him was not the difference between truth and falsehood, but the physiological benefit resulting from one or the other. If downright falsehood promised to be more useful in this respect, he adopted it as the right thing at the right moment, for 'after all, the question is to what end falsehoods are perpetrated'.

Nietzsche never tired of reiterating the fact that men of immutable convictions are of no use whatever when difficult vital problems have to be tackled. 'Convictions are prisons. They never see far enough; they do not look down from a sufficient height; but in order to have any say in questions of value and non-value, a man must have five hundred convictions *beneath* him – behind him. . . . The great passion of a sceptic, the basis and power of his being, which is more enlightened and more despotic than he is himself, enlists all his intellect into its service; it makes him unscrupulous; it even gives him the courage to employ unholy means: in certain circumstances it even allows him convictions. Convictions as a *means*; much is achieved merely by means of a conviction. Great passion makes use of and consumes convictions, it does not submit to them – it knows that it is a sovereign power.' (*The Anti-Christ.*)

The above passage is but a further evidence that to the suffering Nietzsche the problem of 'to be or not to be' mattered more than any stable philosophic truths or systems. And since life happens to be continuous change and becoming, he did not hesitate to base his own philosophy on the same principle and to let 'immutable' theories take care of themselves. Thus he joined a tradition which goes at least as far back as Heraclitus with his dictum that all life is but flux and change. Such a course was required by Nietzsche's 'artifice of self-preservation' which alone was enough to explain most of his apparent whims and eccentricities. Why indeed should he not have indulged in any point of view that promised some strategic advantage, even a temporary one? Was he not free to invoke today the artist against the thinker, and tomorrow the thinker against the artist, if necessary? He even did not mind eulogizing the religious man in order to deride the complacency of the scientist or of a shallow unbeliever. In Nietzsche's own words a 'philosopher who has made the tour of many states of health, and is always making it anew, has also gone through just as many philosophies; he really *cannot* do otherwise than transform his condition on every occasion into the most ingenious posture and position – this art of transformation is philosophy.'

4

As a matter of strategy, once more, Nietzsche instinctively adopted, and had to adopt, the position most likely to summon up the vitality he needed in order to counter his own diseased and decaying body. But here it may perhaps be of some use to make a distinction between strength and vitality. For the two are not identical. Nor are they necessarily found together. Weak and diseased individuals often develop, as though in self-defence, astonishing vitality, the nature of which is psychic rather than physical. To one's surprise they can withstand certain crises better than people with a robust physique. The invalid Nietzsche was not a stranger to this kind of vitality. Fully aware of his condition, he was, as a rule, also the best judge as to what kind of 'vital' attitude he had to summon in order to sustain the tenacity required. In a letter to Georg Brandes he once confessed with candour that his most cheerful book, *The Dawn of Day*, had been written 'in a winter of incredible misery at Genoa, away from doctors, friends and relatives. The book is a sort of dynamo-meter for me: I wrote it with a minimum of health and strength.' In December of the same year (1887) he made an even more startling avowal to Hans von Buelow. 'I will make no mention of the dangerous nature of my emotions,' he wrote to him, 'but this I must say: the altered manner in which I think and feel, and which has been expressed even in my writings during the last six years, has sustained me in life and almost *made* me quite healthy. What do I care if my friends say that my present attitude of a "free spirit" is an eccentric pose, a *resolve* made as it were with clenched teeth, wrung by force and imposed upon my true inclinations? So be it, let all this be my "second nature", but I will yet prove that it is only that second nature that has enabled me to become possessed of my first nature.'

Deliberate self-deception as a means of directing his will along a definite channel, actually became one of his favourite stratagems, but with reservations. He saw quite plainly the inconsistencies inherent in such a method; but he defended them, in the preface to the second edition of his *Human-all-too-Human* (1866), against all possible objections. 'Supposing', he argued, 'that I were reproached with good reasons, what do *you* know, what *could* you know, as to how much artifice of self-preservation, how much rationality and higher protection there is in self-deception – and how much falseness I still require in order to allow myself again and again the luxury of *my* sincerity? . . . In short, I still live; and life, in spite of ourselves, demands illusions, it lives by illusions.' In the same preface he refers to disease itself as an 'instrument and an angling-hook of knowledge. . . . Long years of convalescence may lie in between years full of many-coloured, painfully enchanting magical transformations, curbed and led by a *tough will to health,* which often dares to dress and disguise itself as actual health.'

Nietzsche's 'artifice of self-preservation' thus required continuous vigilance and a series of ruses. At the same time it was also bound to confer something of an exceptional meaning upon the various phases of such a fight with his malady. True enough, a philosophy largely born out of his will to health and affected by that will, was in danger of being narrowed down to a matter of eugenics, food and hygiene – but for Nietzsche's reformatory zeal. He may have raged against dogmatic convictions as distinct from free opinions, but a time came when he, too, began to clamour that '*there should be no doubt* at all concerning all essential values'. Some firm convictions of a sort were thus necessary after all to the defence of life itself.

In his subsequent conception of the will to power he even set up something of a dogma – a physiological dogma of his own – in which he was all the more anxious to believe the more he wanted to counteract the general 'decadence' he had set out to fight. It was here that his ideal of a warrior, full of hardness, came into its own. Yet again it would be misleading to take Nietzsche's utterances about hardness invariably at their face value. They, too, were often masks hiding his true nature which was the opposite of what he pretended it to be. Hence his well-known warning that 'every deep thinker is more afraid of being understood than misunderstood.' Which brings us to some further difficulties he had to cope with and hide behind the many masks provided by his philosophy.

## 5

Viewing health and disease from the angle of their stimulating capacity, Nietzsche eventually simplified his
attitude by welcoming all that could serve what he called
the 'higher health', one's basic or fundamental power of
resistance, no matter how difficult this may have appeared
at times. Having once adopted this method, he had to be
all the more on guard against those moods of despondence
which were likely to obstruct the benefits derived from
his use of philosophy as a self-protective measure. 'Out
of my will to health I made my philosophy. . . . For this
should be thoroughly understood: it was during those years
in which my vitality reached its lowest point that I ceased
to be a pessimist; the instinct of self-recovery forbade my
holding to a philosophy of poverty and desperation.'

One of Nietzsche's merits was the frankness with which
he revealed this secret. But this attitude only increased his
determination to work for that higher capacity which was
designed to confer upon his suffering and struggle a supra-
personal meaning. Unwilling to live the life of an ordinary mortal, he dramatized himself into an exceptional
being in the grand style. He adopted a cause the issue
of which was bound to surpass, in his opinion, any
personal or average destiny. Hence he was the more inclined to look upon the struggle against his own predica-
ments as symbolizing that of Europe, of humanity. Private
ailments of Nietzsche the invalid were thus transmuted
into a matter of general importance. His resistance
was no longer that of an average helpless invalid, but
something much more responsible and remarkable. A
fight of this kind eventually led him to the conviction that
he himself was a destiny on which the outcome of some
crucial dilemma or dilemmas of the age depended. Hence
his determination to be worthy of such a role and to
suppress within himself all those tendencies which
clamoured for a different, a less dramatic or less heroic
personal fate. In short, he became a great enemy of the
line of least resistance not only in theory but also in
practice. What mattered was to be a champion of the

ascending type of life: a task which Nietzsche pursued
relentlessly to the end, regardless of his suffering.

6

It should be mentioned in this context, however, that the
rigorous scrutiny which he applied to the various phases of
his own malady, probably helped Nietzsche to diagnose
certain ailments of 'decaying' Europe better than a
healthier individual might have done. Moreover, having
chosen a severe treatment for himself, he devised, for the
benefit of Europe and indeed of humanity, a therapy
which was even more rigorous than were the counter-
measures he employed against his own illness. Yet
whatever one may think of his remedies, it cannot be
denied that with his sharp eye he detected the root-causes
of many of our modern evils.

In the diseased or decaying body of Europe he concentrated on that process that threatened to dissolve and
destroy the remnants of those cultural values that might
still have been worth preserving. In one of his aphorisms
he summed up the situation in these words: 'The whole of
our culture in Europe has long been writhing in suspense
which increases from decade to decade as in expectation of
a catastrophe, restless, violent, helter-skelter, like a torrent
that will *reach its source*, and refuses to reflect – yea, that
even dreads reflection.' What must have struck him in the
first place was not only the modern 'canting bigotry' with
its lack of any orientation in matters of essential values, but
also the unavoidable commercialization of life, with the
principle of cash and credit installed as the watchful
arbiter over all. The ideal modern *homo sapiens* at practically all social levels was the smug and prosperous
Philistine with his abject 'pleasure for the day' and
'pleasure for the night'. Even the claims of the exploited
masses hardly seemed to go beyond the aspirations towards
universal Philistinism, fairly shared by all.*

* A brief but striking characterization of this type of person can
be found in Zarathustra's sermon under the title, 'The Last Man'
('Der letzte Mensch') in the first part of *Thus Spake Zarathustra.*

One of the reasons behind this situation was that spiritual and moral vacuum which began to overtake the world once the established religions lost their authority. A concurrent and even more fateful cause was the gap between the incredibly accelerated pace of our external – technical and scientific – civilization on the one hand, and the lagging inner or cultural development of modern mankind on the other. In fact, there were hardly any bridges left between the two. Hence quantity prevailed at the expense of quality. Creative culture was being more and more smothered by gigantic industrial productivity. The active external man developed at the expense of the inner man.

This trend in the name of a universal Tower of Babel had found its eloquent sanction in modern politics. Nations competing with each other, jealous of each other, wasted most of their finances, inventions and energies on armaments, ready to start a series of Armageddons at any time and at any price. Imperialism with its aggressive appetites was particularly threatening in Germany, which achieved unification at the very beginning of young Nietzsche's academic and philosophic career. Nietzsche, at first full of admiration for the powerful Bismarckian German Reich, was quick enough to see its flaws: narrow-minded chauvinism with its cult of rattling soldiery and brutal might for its own sake. Squeezed between Russia, France and Great Britain, the German nation was increasingly anxious to enlarge its *Lebensraum* at the expense of its neighbours, and in these efforts it was soon to employ the most ruthless means and methods at its disposal. It may be of some interest that the great poet Heine, who was also a voluntary exile (in Paris), had diagnosed the disturbing latent trends in Germany some three or four decades before Nietzsche. But Heine's vitriolic indictments compare to those of Nietzsche's as the beatings on a drum would compare to the salvos of heavy guns. Moreover, while Heine had condemned only certain aspects of his own epoch, Nietzsche insisted on announcing the twilight descending upon our entire civilization.

The remedies he adopted were drastic. In his opinion they had to be as drastic as the situation he tried to cope with was serious. And so he challenged what he called the 'decadence' of our age and culture with an almost fanatical verve. Yet his very inconsistencies in this struggle were often due not so much to the faults and contradictions of the age he fought against as to the conflicts between the antagonistic traits within his own mind and soul. There were times when he seemed to be not one personality but a mixture of several personalities existing – not quite comfortably – side by side. The most 'godless' philosopher of our age and yet a potential mystic in disguise; a belated romantic of the 'Storm and Stress' brand and, alongside this, an apostle of Apollo – the god of discipline, harmony and measure; a preacher of hardness and harshness in theory, and one of the meekest of men in practice – these and other incongruous features jostled each other in his complex personality. Elements of Pascal, Luther, Goethe, Voltaire and the poet Hölderlin seemed to have met in Nietzsche not as allies but as rivals vainly trying to adjust to each other. In his effort to preserve at least the semblance of a balance between his contradictory traits he often 'cast the skin' and shifted the focus of his attention from one element to another; but every attempt of this kind only added yet another mask to his series of disguises. Little wonder that Nietzsche himself warned his readers against those ideological 'apes' who confuse the mask with the man at the risk of missing both.

## 7

A great deal of Nietzsche's originality was due precisely to the way he combined his own personal diagnosis with the one he applied to the Europe of his time. And since his aim in both cases was living life, he could not help developing a number of aspects of that 'existentialism' whose postulate is that philosophy should arise out of life itself, with the problem of man's existence and man's fate as the kernel of it. And here he knew how to be merciless in his judgements – merciless in the service of life.

'A philosopher must be the evil conscience of his age,'
he once said, 'but to this end he must be possessed of its
best knowledge.' Nietzsche's way of reaching this
knowledge was not confined to his mental concepts alone.
Unable and unwilling to divorce philosophy from life, he
subordinated his *Erkennen* (knowledge through intellect)
to his own *Erleben* (living experience). He himself states in
*The Joyful Wisdom* that 'it makes the most material
difference whether a thinker is personally related to his
problems, having his fate, his need, his highest happiness
therein; or impersonally, being only able to grasp them
with the tentacles of coldly prying thinking'. And again,
'We philosophers are not at liberty to separate soul and
body, as common folk separate them; and we are still less
at liberty to separate soul and spirit. We are not thinking
frogs, we are not objectifying and registering apparatuses
with cold entrails – our thoughts must be continually born
out of pain, and we must, motherlike, share with them all
that we have in us of blood, heart, ardour, joy, passion,
pangs, conscience, fate and fatality. Life – that means for
us to transform constantly into light and flame, all that we
are and all that we meet with; we cannot possibly do
otherwise.' No existentialist philosopher could have put
it more succinctly and clearly.

While realizing that a philosophy which has to be lived
and tested through one's personal fate is often likely to
appear as incongruous as life itself, Nietzsche knew that its
very contradictions may often prove to be more vital and
therefore more valuable than any abstract systems
reasoned out in a comfortable armchair. And since he was
determined to be the 'evil conscience of his age', he was not
in the least afraid of acknowledging that he himself, too,
was one of its products – a product as decadent indeed as
the age itself, but with a difference.

'Apart from the fact that I am a decadent, I am also the
reverse of such a creature. That energy with which I
sentenced myself to absolute solitude, and to a severance
from all those conditions of life to which I had grown
accustomed; my discipline of myself, and my refusal to

allow myself to be pampered, to be tended hand and foot, to be doctored – all this betrays the absolute certainty of my instincts respecting what at that time was most needful to my health. This double thread of experience, this means to two worlds that seem so far asunder, finds in every detail its counterpart in my own nature; I am my own complement; I have a second sight, as well as a first. And perhaps I have also a third sight.'

Nietzsche wrote these words in his last book, *Ecce Homo* (1888); but he could have written them at any time, since the theme of a struggle between a 'decadent' and the 'reverse of such a creature' runs through the whole of his life and work. After all, it was not for nothing that he wrote at the same time to Malwida von Meysenbug: 'In questions of decadence I am now the highest authority on earth.' Each of his books marks in fact a certain stage reached in the duel between the two interior antagonists. No sooner had he discovered a 'decadent' trait within himself than he invented its antidote. And since, from 1879 in particular, his ailments kept increasing, he learned soon enough how to increase his challenge and defiance accordingly. His biography reveals numerous examples of how often he indulged in deliberate hardness towards himself as a contrast and compensation to his innate gentleness. He was in fact so offended by actual hardness and cruelty that when, on 3 January 1889 in Turin, he saw a coachman whipping an old horse, he sobbingly embraced the animal and then fainted – an episode which hastened his mental collapse. Even his apotheosis of the 'will to power' was – in some of its aspects – but another compensation on the part of a helpless invalid. Whatever his theoretical pronouncements, in practice he could be hard only to himself and never to others.

Nietzsche's friendship and subsequent quarrel with Richard Wagner are particularly significant in this respect. He often said that the years of friendship with Wagner had been the happiest of his life. This was certainly true of those Tribschen days when the young Professor Nietzsche used to spend one weekend after the other with

Wagner and Cosima. Yet soon after his visits to Bayreuth
in 1876 he suddenly gave him up without any regard for
his own feelings. This breach, as well as his later savage
attacks upon Wagner's music, caused a number of rumours
and misrepresentation. Some people saw base motives in
the rift, or even jealousy on the part of Nietzsche, who also
happened to be a talented musician and sometimes com-
posed himself. A more likely explanation is the view that
his attacks on Wagner were first of all attacks on those
'Wagnerian' propensities as well as temptations which he
had felt so strongly within himself but now considered
utterly negative. In October 1868, some eight years before
his quarrel with Wagner, Nietzsche wrote to his friend
Erwin Rohde: 'My pleasure in Wagner is much the same
as my pleasure in Schopenhauer: the ethical air, the
redolence of Faust and also the Cross – death and the
tomb.'

In short, his early delight in Wagner's music had been
above all the delight of a romantic decadent à la mode.
Yet having come to the conclusion that in serving Wagner
he was paying homage to decadence itself, he turned
against Wagner as resolutely as he could. In attacking
Wagner, Nietzsche the philosopher and physician thus
attacked Nietzsche the ailing 'decadent'. And this despite
the fact that in his affliction he was certainly aware of the
fact that he needed Wagner's music as a soothing narcotic.*
The temptation to indulge in it was made stronger by his
personal attachment to the composer who must have been,
with all his defects, a fascinating personality. So Nietzsche
had either to break the spell or be broken by it. He decided
to break it. But the real motive behind such a step can be
gauged from this line in the letter he wrote to Peter Gast
on 25 July 1882: 'With true horror did I realize how closely
related I was to Wagner.' And on 3 February 1883, he
confessed to the same correspondent: 'I am better, and
even believe that Wagner's death was the most substantial

* In the autumn of 1888 he wrote in the autobiographic *Ecce
Homo*: 'If a man wishes to get rid of a feeling of insufferable
oppression, he has to take hashish. Well, I had to take Wagner.'

relief that could have been given me just now. It was hard to be for six years an opponent of the man whom I had most reverenced on earth, and my constitution is not coarse enough for such a position.'

Deliberate hardness against some of his strongest inclinations thus formed the very basis of Nietzsche's auto-therapy, or lived philosophy, if you prefer to call it so. Whenever he detected in himself any symptoms of weakness such as pessimism, despondence, the wish to be 'soothed', the craving for rest and resignation, he immediately took counter-measures of the severest kind. There were times when he toyed with his own 'decadence' like a cat playing with a mouse before killing it. But on the other hand such inner warfare kept him on the alert and stimulated the remnants of his vitality. 'War has always been the great policy of all spirits who have penetrated too far into themselves, or have grown too deep; a wound stimulates the recuperative powers.' Feeding, after each wound, on his 'recuperative powers', Nietzsche was always ready to challenge any negative feature in his own physical and mental make-up. The war within his split conscious-ness thus grew increasingly fierce. A time came in fact, when he began to consider the harshest aspects of reality as a test of his endurance, for which purpose he was quite ready to welcome them. Among his last aphorisms, for instance, one can find passages such as this: 'How much truth can a spirit endure? *For how much truth is it daring enough?* This for me was a real measure of value.' And again: 'The kind of *experimental* philosophy which I am living even anticipates the possibility of the most funda-mental nihilism on principle.' To which he yet immediately adds: 'By this I do not mean that it remains standing at a negation. It would rather attain to the very reverse.' (*The Will to Power*.)

This suggests, however, a further important conclusion; for it is here that we meet again Nietzsche's conception of the 'tragic individual' as distinct from, or even the opposite of, a mere pessimist. The difference lies above all in the direction of one's will. Whereas the pessimist either

runs away from reality to various 'comforts' or else falls a
prey to nihilistic negation, the tragic seeker after knowledge
is ready to compel his spirit (*Geist*) 'to perceive *against*
its own inclination and often enough against the wishes of
his heart: he forces it to say Nay, where he would like to
affirm, love and adore; indeed every instance of taking a
thing profoundly and fundamentally is a violation, an
intentional injuring of the fundamental will of the spirit,
which instinctively aims at appearance and superficiality;
even in every desire for knowledge there is a drop of
cruelty.' This is what he says in *Beyond Good and Evil*.
But the price one has to pay for this is suffering. A self-
knower thus often becomes a self-torturer, a 'self-
hangman' –

> Mid a hundred mirrors
> False to thyself,
> Mid a hundred memories
> Uncertain
> Weary at every wound,
> Shivering at every frost,
> Throttled in thine own noose,
> Self-knower!
> Self-Hangman!
>
> ..      ..      ..
>
> Thou soughtest the heaviest burden –
> So foundest thyself,
> And canst not shake thyself off. . . .*

## 8

We thus arrive at the opposite end of all soothing comfort.
But even the pain which such a 'self-hangman' cannot or
does not want to shake off may pass into pride. The very
amount of endurance may here become a measure of one's
pride, especially when the struggle itself is also considered
a defence of life as a whole. Nietzsche, who was always
ready to look upon the struggle with himself in precisely
this light, could not but interpret his personal case

* *Dionysian Dithyrambs* (1888).

symbolically, identifying his own 'decadence' with that of the age in which he lived. Hence he was logically compelled to apply his personal remedies to it: to prove, as it were, through himself that contemporary mankind might be healed if properly treated. An attitude of this sort made him less than ever willing to falter or to capitulate, no matter how great the trials he had to endure. Any weakness or cowardice in this respect would have been a betrayal not only of his own life but of life as a whole. And as for the temptations of suicide, that would be the acme of weakness.

The very tension of such a situation may show to the tragic individual even pain itself in such a new light as to enable him to 'withstand all the seductiveness of suicide and to make the continuation of life seem very desirable to the sufferer. His mind scornfully turns against the warm and comfortable dream-world in which the healthy man moves about thoughtlessly, and he thinks with contempt of the noblest and most cherished illusions in which he formerly indulged. He experiences delight in conjuring up this contempt as if from the depths of hell, and thus inflicting the bitterest sufferings upon his soul; it is by this counterpoise that he bears up against physical suffering – he feels that such a counterpoise is essential! ... Our pride revolts as it never did before, it experiences an incomparable charm in defending life against such a tyrant. In this state of mind we take up a bitter stand against all pessimism in order that it may not appear to be a consequence of our condition, and thus humiliate us as conquered ones. The charm of being just in our judgement was also never greater than now; it is now, if ever, that we wish to show that we need no excuse. We pass through downright orgies of pride.' (*The Dawn of Day*.)

These 'orgies of pride' kept growing in Nietzsche, especially from *The Joyful Wisdom* onwards, and made him regard all craving for pleasure or happiness as a high road towards weakness or even spiritual slavery. His ideal became the true warrior: free, virile, and full of contempt for easy comfort. The measure of freedom itself became, in his opinion, above all the resistance which had to be overcome in order to 'remain uppermost'.

Nietzsche, in whom this warrior-ideal had developed through his own pain and suffering, could not help postulating (by analogy) pain and suffering as something desirable or even necessary for mankind at large. This is why he was so fond of ridiculing the utilitarian slogans about the 'greatest happiness of the greatest number'. In his vocabulary hedonism was but another name for decay. Hence his challenge to those propensities, whether Christian, democratic or humanitarian, whose aim is to diminish or even to do away with suffering and the inner resistance awakened by it. In this manner Nietzsche's defence of life actually amounted to Spartan severity or even cruelty with regard to life as it is. Instead of diminishing suffering, he wanted to turn it into a vigorous creative discipline or self-discipline of man.

Yet, paradoxically, in the very teeth of his heroically exaggerated cult of suffering Nietzsche himself had been constantly searching for some relief from his own predicament through success in love. The quest reached its culmination in his strange emotional entanglement with Lou Salomé – a crucial experience perhaps best understood against the background of his emotional life in general.

# 3 Nietzsche and love

As in so many other things, Nietzsche was ambiguous in his attitude towards women. The rough tones he often adopted when writing about them should never be taken too literally. There was a frustrated romantic behind it, even a sentimental dreamer, much too shy to be a ladies' man let alone a heart-breaker. The women he felt more at home with were elderly spinsters (but not of the 'bluestocking' variety) in whose company sex hardly mattered. How much he really yearned for that kind of loyal care which only a woman could have given him was shown by his attachment to his self-reliant and bossy sister Elisabeth whose help he needed and made use of precisely because she was so different from him: practical, calculatingly prudent, and even unscrupulous when necessary.

This need for feminine companionship grew stronger in him from his Basle years on. In October 1874 he wrote to Malwida von Meysenbug, 'What I wish at present, I tell you confidentially, is to have as soon as possible a good wife.' But since he failed to make any woman of the right kind fall in love with him, he found it necessary to interpret his lack of success so as to remain 'favourably inclined' towards himself. His pride and egotism would not admit that the fault was his own, so it had to be on the other side. Thus in his *Human, all-too-Human* he argues aphoristically that 'women always intrigue against the higher souls of their husbands; they want to cheat them out of their future for the sake of a painless and comfortable present.' Yet this is mild compared with what he has to say about women in *Thus Spake Zarathustra*, for example, where he assumes an almost oriental attitude.

'Men shall be trained for war, and women for the recreation of the warrior; all else is folly.'

'The happiness of man is, "I will". The happiness of a woman is, "he will".'

'Thou goest to women? Do not forget the whip!'

Not much is known about Nietzsche's early sexual life, but it is almost certain that he had to pay a terrible price for indiscriminate contacts with women.* The extract from the log of the Jena clinic has already been quoted. Again, in the records of the Basle hospital where Nietzsche was under treatment in the first half of January 1889 it states that Nietzsche admitted having become infected 'on two previous occasions'. And Dr Baumann, who had examined Nietzsche in Turin at the outbreak of his insanity, wrote in his report: 'Maintains that he is a famous man, and is asking for women all the time.'

2

If Nietzsche's illness and subsequent insanity were due to syphilitic infection (a supposition which – for obvious reasons – could hardly have been unanimously endorsed), his outbursts against women can be understood. But once he had worked out his scheme of things with the superman as its apex, he could not relegate to woman the role of a mere female and 'recreation of the warrior'. After all, the prospective superman had the right to demand that at least his mother should be a woman worthy of giving birth to such a wonder. Aware of this, Nietzsche proceeded to depict in glowing terms the mother of the superman as he would like her to be. Yet in the same *Thus Spake Zarathustra* we find images as voluptuous as if they had emanated from an eastern potentate surrounded by a swarm of odalisques. The dithyramb 'Among the Daughters of the Desert' might well have been written by a man whose unsatisfied sexuality looked for extra-strong compensatory fantasies. However, we must be on our guard when Nietzsche poses as an 'experienced' connoisseur of women. Many of his spiteful references about them emanated from Schopenhauer or the French *philosophes*

* In the winter of 1876, while staying, with Rée and Peter Gast, as Malwida's guest in a villa at Sorrento on the gulf of Naples, Nietzsche made (according to Rée) frequent nightly visits to a local peasant girl.

of the eighteenth century. The fury of his attacks is, moreover, suggestive of a bachelor in whom the craving for the loving woman has been repressed but not suppressed. Yet as chance would have it, even in his early Basle days Nietzsche was in contact with a woman he was able to admire and secretly love – Cosima Wagner.

Nietzsche saw Cosima regularly at Tribschen during his friendship with Richard Wagner. His notes and correspondence testify to the deep impression she made upon him. It is quite possible that one of the subconscious causes of Nietzsche's breach with Wagner in 1876 was his admiration for Cosima. Hence the invectives Nietzsche hurled, later on, at his one-time friend whom he suddenly wanted to unmask as being a *Falschmuenzer* (forger) of music, a *poseur*, and a compendium of all decadent vices. Was Nietzsche anxious to prove to the world, and above all to Cosima herself, that of the two rivals for her love Wagner was decidedly unworthy of her, even though he was her lord and master? Yet as late as the autumn of 1888 the same Nietzsche in *Ecce Homo* was able to make such an acknowledgement as: 'I would not have the days I spent at Tribschen – those days of confidence, of cheerfulness, of sublime flashes, and of profound moments – blotted from my life at any price. I do not know what Wagner may have been for others; but no cloud ever darkened *our* sky.'

After his breach with Richard Wagner Nietzsche never saw Cosima again. But he did not get rid of Cosima's image – the image of the woman who might perhaps have helped him to come to terms with himself, with his task, and with life in general, had she loved him and not Wagner. All this remained of course in the realm of frustrated wishes and day-dreams. With a kind of rancorous musing Nietzsche was even inclined to think that the disparity between Cosima and Wagner was one of the causes of Wagner's artistic 'ruin'. In 1887, less than two years before his collapse, he wrote in his notebook: 'Frau Cosima Wagner is the only woman made in a great style I have ever met, but I grudge her the fact that she ruined

Wagner. How could such a thing have happened? He
was unworthy of such a wife: and so in gratitude he
became her victim [zum Dank dafür verfiel er ihr].'

3

Cosima was not the only love of Nietzsche's Basle period.
During the festivals at Bayreuth, in 1876, he met a certain
Mme Louise Ott – a charming Parisienne of Slav extraction who made a strong impression upon him, but who
was already happily married. Nietzsche's attitude towards
her was chivalrous, while his letters to her were affectionate
and full of respect. Thus on 29 August 1877 he addressed
her in a letter from Engadine as 'dear friend', declaring
that: 'I shall not forsake my mountain loneliness without
once more writing to tell you how fond I am of you. How
superfluous it is to say this, or to write it, isn't it? But my
affection for anyone sticks to them like a thorn, and at
times is as troublesome as a thorn; it is not easy to get rid
of it. So be good enough to receive this small, superfluous,
and troublesome letter.

'A day or two ago, quite suddenly, I saw your eyes in the
dark. Why does no one ever look at me with such eyes? I
exclaimed irritably. Oh, it is ghastly.'

In the same year he was introduced at Geneva to
Mathilde Trampedach – a girl from the Baltic provinces
in Russia – and evidently fell in love with her. This time
he made a proposal in writing, but was rejected. As
though wounded in his pride, he retired within himself.
But on hearing of Rohde's happy marriage, he sent him on
28 August 1877 the following pathetic lines: 'When, a day
or two ago, someone told me, "Rohde's young wife is an
exceedingly sweet woman whose every feature is illumined
by her noble soul", I actually wept. And I can give you no
plausible reason for having done so. We might ask the
psychologists for an explanation. Ultimately they would
declare it was envy and that I grudge you your happiness.'

Five years later, when he met in Rome 'die interessante
Russin', Lou Salomé, he once more ventured to take a
woman seriously. During his walks and talks with her he

came to the conclusion that he had found not only a lovable friend but also a disciple (he could never quite separate the two), and perhaps a wonderful companion for life. Daily conversations seemed to prove that she was the right choice for him, although he must have been aware that his good friend, Rée, was also in love with her. Dr Paul Rée had published some years previously (in 1877) the book, *About the Origins of Moral Sentiments* (*Der Ursprung der Moralischen Empfindungen*), which was strongly approved by Nietzsche. He even referred in a pun to the influence of Rée-alism upon his own second period – Nietzsche was a past master at making puns. In contrast to the invalid Nietzsche, with his meagre pension hardly enough to cover his own needs, of an 'eternal refugee', the young philosopher Rée was a man in good health and of independent means. On the other hand, Rée suffered from an incurable feeling of inferiority which was in the end his undoing.

Lou found in Nietzsche a kindred spirit grappling with problems which appealed to her enormously. This made her all the more determined to continue her studies abroad – despite the fact that her mother had come from St Petersburg to Rome in order to take her daughter back to Russia. Obstinate and strong-willed in the extreme, Lou did not find it too difficult to override her mother's objections. She moreover played with the eccentric scheme of a study-trio consisting of herself, Rée and Nietzsche, all of whom would share the same flat in Vienna or in some other city, as the case might be. The immediate consequences of all these encounters and friendships, however, soon became more hectic than expected.

In early May 1882, Lou, her mother, Nietzsche and Rée left Rome and went together to the little old town of Orta by the lake of the same name. Lou and Nietzsche had a number of friendly walks together, exploring the environs, both of them enjoying the intoxicating spring atmosphere. It was during one of those excursions *à deux* that Lou seems to have given the enamoured philosopher some minutes which made him exceedingly happy. So

much so that when, soon after that, they all went to
Lucerne, Nietzsche made another proposal (this time
without an intermediary) to Lou – but again to no
purpose.* Still, Nietzsche continued to love and to hope.
He even invited Lou to come and spend the summer in his
company at Tautenburg in Thuringia – a plan which she
gladly accepted. In order to make things easier for her and
eliminate unnecessary gossip, Nietzsche wrote to his sister
asking her to meet Lou and come together with her to
Tautenburg as her chaperon. At the same time it was
arranged that Lou's mother should stay as a guest of Rée's
parents on their estate in West Prussia.

In June Lou attended the Wagner festival at Bayreuth
where she met Elisabeth. The encounter however was far
from being friendly. Elisabeth (who was fourteen years
older than the Russian girl, began, rather tactlessly, to talk
down to Lou as a schoolmistress might to an immature
pupil, at which Lou simply laughed. A violent quarrel
ensued, but the two women made peace of a sort and went
together to the village in the Tautenburg forest where
Nietzsche was waiting for them. There Lou spent about a
month, during which she saw much of Nietzsche and had
many stimulating discussions with him, even though
Elisabeth tried hard to lower his esteem for her. She was
of course jealous of Lou's influence over Nietzsche, and,
in addition, her own provincial respectability could not
tolerate the Russian girl's free way of life. 'My sister
regards Lou as a poisonous beast which should be des-
troyed whatever the cost, and she behaves accordingly',
Nietzsche wrote to Malwida von Meysenbug.

Conflicts and ugly family quarrels became unavoidable.
As a result Nietzsche's enthusiasm for Lou (with the
possible implication of marriage) led to a breach with his
sister and his rather conventional and simple-minded

* There exists a strange photograph of Lou and her two
friends, taken while they were in Lucerne: Lou sits in a tiny
farm cart whose shaft is held by Nietzsche and Rée as if they
were two harnessed domestic animals. The whip in Lou's hand
seems to indicate her independence of any whims except her own.

mother. During this period he regarded himself as Lou's secret fiancé and was obviously thinking of turning a new leaf in his life: he intended to take up some research connected particularly with the problems of Eternal Recurrence – an idea which he referred to in a letter to Rohde on 15 July 1882: 'In the autumn I am going to the University of Vienna to begin student life afresh, after having made somewhat of a failure of my old life, thanks to a one-sided study of philology. Now I have my own plan of study and behind it my own secret goal to which the remaining years of my life are consecrated. I find it *too hard* to live if I cannot do so in the *grand style* – this in confidence to you, my old comrade. Without a goal that I could regard as inexpressibly important I should not have been able to hold myself aloft in the light above the black flood.' A proof of Nietzsche's own influence over Lou is provided by her German poem, *A Prayer to Life* (*Gebet an das Leben*) which she wrote in those days and which Nietzsche set to music as soon as he received it. Such lines as these could have been written by himself:

> Lass deine Flamme meinen Geist entzünden,
> Lass der Glut des Kampfes mich
> Die Rätsellösung deines Wesens finden,
> Jahrtausende zu denken und zu leben,
> Wirf deinen Inhalt voll hinein –
> Hast du kein Glück mehr übrig mir zu geben,
> Wohlan, noch hast du deine Pein.

> (Let thy flame my spirit kindle,
> Let me in the glow of strife
> Find the solution of thy enigmatic essence,
> Let me think and live a thousand years,
> Throw all thy contents wholly into it –
> Hast thou no happiness left to give me,
> Well, thou canst still give me thy Pain.)

In October Lou, Nietzsche and Rée met in Leipzig. Angered by his family's opposition to Lou, Nietzsche hoped that she at any rate would not be too much affected by it. Nor did he give up the idea that she might join

him and share his studies – no longer in Vienna this time,
but in Paris. Meanwhile Lou and Rée had left for Berlin,
and this only increased Elisabeth's antagonism to her rival.
Slander and gossip soon reached such proportions that
they began to have a deleterious effect on Nietzsche's
state of mind. Hints at a *liaison* between Lou and Rée
drove him into such a state that he considered challenging
Rée to a duel. His friendship with both Lou and Rée came
to an abrupt end and for a time he seemed to be on the
verge of suicide, but again his 'recuperative power' saved
him.

4

Nietzsche was thirty-eight years old when he parted from
Lou never to see her again. Nothing reliable is known
about his love life from that time on. What is certain is the
fact that losing Lou was a great ordeal for him, the more so
as it transpired that in 1883 Lou and Rée actually lived
together for a time, though in all probability not as man
and wife. Nietzsche's subsequent admirer, the Danish
literary historian Georg Brandes, acknowledged in a
letter (17 December 1887) that during a stay in Berlin he
had met a Dr Rée who was living 'according to his own
account on purely platonic terms' with an intelligent
Russian woman – Lou Salomé.

After such a blow to his hopes the only course left for
Nietzsche was to forget Lou, or at least to convince
himself that the matter was so much below his taste and
dignity as to be unworthy even of his hatred. He came to
terms with mother and sister, sending to Elisabeth at the
end of August 1883, a letter in which he desperately tried
to prove that he had already risen far above the episode
which had cost him and others so much trouble: 'What do
these Rées and Lous matter!' he wrote. 'How can I be
their enemy? And even if they had harmed me, I have
surely derived enough benefit from them, if only from the
fact that they are people of such different order from
myself; in this I find complete compensation – aye, even a
reason for feeling grateful to them both. They both seem

to be original people and not copies, and that is why I suffered their company, however distasteful they were to me.'

In spite of these reassuring utterances he was in such a state of mind and nerves as to be unable to sleep unless he took chloral hydrate, opium and other drugs which could not but further impair his health. Hence it was all the easier for his sister Elisabeth to regain, step by step, her mastery over him. Knowing full well how much her brother needed a woman's care and solicitude, she did her best to be his friend and confidante, even a substitute for a thoughtful wife, but on her own terms. In 1884 she married Bernard Foerster, a notorious anti-Semite who had founded an abortive German settlement (Nueva Germania) in Paraguay with the object of colonizing and – perhaps – even Germanizing that part of the country. Elisabeth joined her husband in South America, but this did not diminish her hold over her brother with whom she was in correspondence all the time. After her husband's suicide in June 1889 she stayed on in Paraguay for another six years and continued his work, hopeless though it must have looked.

Lou Salomé, too, had a chequered existence after the disturbing Tautenburg affair. Whatever her entanglements with Rée, they did not prevent her from embarking upon quite a successful literary career. At the age of twenty-three she wrote her first autobiographic novel, *In a Struggle for God* (*Im Kampf um Gott*), which was well received when it appeared in 1885. Incidentally, she portrayed in this psychological novel both Nietzsche and Rée. Among her numerous subsequent books and essays, her study *Frederick Nietzsche in His Works* (*Friedrich Nietzsche in seinen Werken.* 1894) and another autobiographic novel *Ruth* (1895) established her reputation in the literary world of the day.

In 1887 she married the German orientalist Friedrich Carl Andreas, who eventually became a professor at Goettingen University; but as far as one knows, this marriage was never consummated. On the other hand, in

those very years she met several men who were able to
awaken her retarded and inhibited sexual feeling; but Dr
Rée was evidently not one of them.* While busily engaged
in her literary activities, Lou often used to leave her
husband for long periods in order to associate herself with
men in whose work she shared an interest. Thus, when in
1897 she met the Austrian poet Rainer Maria Rilke in
Munich, she became his mistress for over three years. She
not only taught him Russian (Rilke actually wrote six
poems in Russian), but initiated him into some deeper
aspects of the Russian mind and spirit. This explains a
number of Russian motifs in Rilke's poetry, beginning
with his superb *Book of Hours* (*Stundenbuch*). In 1911
Lou Andreas-Salomé, as she called herself after her
marriage, joined the psychoanalytical circle of Sigmund
Freud, who had a high opinion of her and for a while she
practised psychotherapy successfully. She died in 1937.

## 5

After his disappointment with Lou, Nietzsche abandoned any serious idea of marriage. He did this even while
realizing that a housewife (if nothing more) might perhaps
bring some order into his helplessly roaming existence.
When, in 1888, his now distant sister (or Lama, as he
called her affectionately) alluded in one of her letters from
South America to the possibility of his getting married, he
replied to her (25 January 1888) as follows: 'You can take
my word for it, that for men like me, a marriage after the
type of Goethe's would be the best of all – that is to say, a
marriage with a good housekeeper! But even this idea is
repellent to me. A young and cheerful daughter to whom
I would be an object of reverence would be much more to
the point. The best of all, however, would be my good old
Lama again. For a philosopher a sister is an excellent
philanthropic institution, particularly when she is bright,
and loving, but as a rule one only recognizes this when it is
too late.' Whatever his former conflicts with Elisabeth, he
missed her more than ever precisely because she was so

* He committed suicide in 1901.

inaccessible. True enough, during the weeks of his stay in Nice from where he sent that letter to her, Nietzsche was frequently seen in the company of a young lady with whom he took a number of walks. But her identity remained unknown. All one can say is that in spite of his assertions to the contrary, the need for a woman's love and affection kept smouldering in the deeper layers of his consciousness.

An eloquent illustration of this is his fragment *Naxos*, jotted down in 1885. Here Nietzsche actually constructed of Cosima, Richard Wagner and himself a mythological trio in which Cosima figures as Ariadne, Wagner as the caddish Theseus, and Nietzsche himself as Dionysus who magnanimously marries Ariadne after Theseus, like a coward, has deserted her at Naxos. 'Last act. Marriage of Dionysus and Ariadne' . . . His hidden wishful thinking is clear. Three years later, when his mind broke down, he sent to Cosima three notes, in the second of which he addressed her as Ariadne: '*Ariadne, ich liebe dich*' ('Ariadne, I love you'). And among the disconnected gibberish recorded during his stay at the Jena clinic appears this exclamation, (27 March 1889): 'My wife, Cosima Wagner, has brought me here.'

The aftermath of Nietzsche's affair with Lou soon resulted in another proof of his psychic and mental recuperative power. For in the winter of the same year he was already able to begin writing his principal work, *Thus Spake Zarathustra*—a dazzling introduction to his third period which was full of such creative activities that their very intensity was bound to hasten his catastrophe. Yet it is almost impossible to appreciate the personal and supra-personal aspects of his *magnum opus* unless one first examines some of those inner as well as external difficulties which he had to cope with in order to complete this gospel with its 'glad tidings' from the other, that is anti-religious, end.

# 4 Anti-Religion

Nowhere is the inner split in Nietzsche more evident than in matters of religion. In this respect, too, his *conscious attitude* was entirely different from his *unconscious propensities* inherited from three generations of pious Protestant pastors. As a boy Nietzsche was nicknamed by his comrades 'der kleine Pastor' ('the little pastor') – a hint that even at that age he intended to follow the example of his forbears. According to his sister's testimony, Nietzsche was a very pious child and gave much thought to religious questions, which, as she puts it, he was always anxious to convert into practice. Among the poems he wrote in the winter of 1863–4, while still a pupil at Pforta, there is one under the title *To the Unknown God* which speaks for itself:

> Once more, before my vision turns
> To strange horizons, untried lands,
> To Thee I lift my lonely hands
> For whom my spirit yearns,
>
> To whom, within its ultimate shrine,
> Are solemn altars dedicate,
> While yet I wait
> The summoning voice to claim me Thine.
>
> Thereon is writ in characters ablaze
> The deep-cut legend, 'To the Unknown God';
> For His am I, although my feet have trod,
> Even to this hour, in foul and miry ways.
>
> Yea, I will know Thee, great Unknown,
> Who shakest the foundations of my soul.
> Urgent and clamorous as the thunder's roll,
> Eternally apart, eternally my own.
> Yea, I will know Thee – I will serve Thee.*

* Translated by Rose Fyleman.

On entering Bonn University, Nietzsche registered for both classics and theology, since at that time he was still fully under the influence of German Protestantism. Gradually, however, the vision of ancient Hellas on the one hand and the spell of Schopenhauer's philosophy on the other became such an overpowering inner experience with him that he tried to blend the two. Both the romantic 'Cross' (mentioned in his letter to Erwin Rohde in 1868), and the cult of Wagner, influenced his feelings. Then, however, he adopted that biological outlook which he could in no way reconcile with his inherited Christian religion. Yet even after having condemned Christianity wholesale, he still retained his profound religious instinct which played havoc with him on many occasions. As late as 1881 he wrote to Peter Gast: 'Whatever I may say about Christianity, I cannot forget that I owe to it the best experiences of my spiritual life; and I hope that at the bottom of my heart I'll never be ungrateful to it.' Moreover, the very name of Zarathustra would hardly have been chosen by Nietzsche had he not felt a certain affinity with that old Persian sage and founder of a religion.

Nietzsche himself was by nature a potential founder of a religion: something which had been acutely perceived by Lou Salomé. And however much he may have asserted his own individual self, his innate propensity towards religious universalism broke through repeatedly and at times in full measure. If ever there was a man endowed with a capacity for warm, all-embracing love, that man was Nietzsche. In the jottings for his *Dawn of Day*, we find the following eloquent passage: 'All the time I am dominated by the idea that my fate is not merely personal; that I am doing something for many if I live and develop in this way; I always feel as though I myself were a multitude (*Mehrheit*) which I address in a confidential, earnest and comforting manner.' Or take these few lines, typical of the hidden mystical strain in him: 'The first question is by no means whether we are satisfied with ourselves, but whether we are satisfied with the rest of things at all. Granting that we should say Yea to any single moment,

we have then affirmed not only ourselves, but the whole of
existence. For nothing stands by itself, either in us or in
other things: and if our soul has vibrated and rung with
happiness, like a chord, once only and only once, then all
eternity was necessary in order to bring about that one
event – and all eternity, in this single moment of our
affirmation, was called good, was saved, justified and
blessed.' (*The Joyful Wisdom.*)

Nietzsche's misanthropy came not from any incapacity
for love and sympathy in a deeper sense, but from the fact
that he was unable to love what he could not at the same
time respect and admire. All his friendships were regulated
by the amount of esteem he felt for the person or persons
concerned. The isolation he felt with regard to his contemporaries was due, apart from his malady, to his inveterate
propensity to transfer his sympathies to ghosts and
phantoms of his own making rather than bow to those
humans he saw about him. Unable to admire others, he
was all the more tempted to admire his own different and –
as he thought – superior self. Yet this, too, was only an
ambiguous compensation for his thwarted impulse to
expand, to give of his very best in the sense described in
Zarathustra's passages about 'Bestowing Virtue'*:

'Uncommon is the highest virtue, and unprofiting;
beaming is it, and soft of lustre, a bestowing virtue is the
highest virtue.

'Verily, I divine you well, my disciples: ye strive like me
for bestowing virtue. What should ye have in common with
cats and wolves?

'It is your thirst to become sacrifices and gifts your-
selves: and therefore have ye the thirst to accumulate all
riches in your soul.

'Insatiably striveth your soul for treasures and jewels
because your virtue is insatiable in desiring to bestow.

'Ye constrain all things to flow towards you and into

---

* 'Die schenkende Tugend' in the original. What Nietzsche
meant by it was the kind of generosity which is rich enough to
want and to be able to give or 'bestow', out of its own overflowing
abundance.

you, so that they shall flow back again out of your fountain
as the gifts of your love.

'Upwards goes our course from genera to genera. But a
horror to us is the degenerating sense, which says: 'All
for myself!'

2

In this manner Nietzsche filled even his 'physiological'
outlook with a religious-moral pathos, although the two
planes may contradict or even exclude each other. But at
the same time he repudiated any belief in God, in Providence and in a world 'beyond', no matter how cruelly such
a step may have clashed with some of his secret needs and
desires. 'The seeker of knowledge operates as an artist and
glorifier of cruelty in that he compels his spirit to perceive
against its own inclination and often enough against the
wishes of his heart: he forces it to say Nay where he
would like to affirm, love and adore.' (*Beyond Good and
Evil.*)

It was the repressed Christian within him who spoke
these words. Yet in the state he was in he could hardly have
acted otherwise without weakening his will to health and
jeopardizing his self-imposed therapy. In spite of the
wishes of his heart, he persisted in 'cruelty' towards
himself, or even self-inquisition, as he called it. So he
turned his back on all religion, suppressing his strong
religious temperament. He did not want to know how far
such and such a religion was true, but whether it was
valuable or harmful from the standpoint of an ascending
type of life. And no sooner had he noticed its emphasis on
the 'beyond' at the expense of our earthly existence than
he rejected it as being of no value at all. The same applies
to the problem of God. Even had he been sure that God
existed, the invalid Nietzsche would not have accepted
Him unless God first produced credentials to the effect
that He was not hostile to life, that is, to our 'biological'
life this side of the grave.

It is here that we must look for the roots of Nietzsche's
attacks upon religion, and particularly Christianity, in

which he had detected (or thought he had detected) all the
elements of nihilism and decadence. The first proof of
these he saw in the hypocritical and lukewarm attitude
towards religion on the part of the Christians themselves
– an attitude which he regarded as infinitely more
demoralizing than honest atheism. To call oneself
Christian, when the whole of life is in practice one continuous refutation of Christianity was, according to him,
the height of indecency and moral cowardice at its worst.
Such a state of things he could only despise. Neither
Christianity nor a God of this kind was of any use to him,
and he was frank about it.

'That which separates us from other people', he argued
in one of his last books, *The Anti-Christ* (*Der Antichrist*,
1888), 'is not the fact that we can discover no God in
either history or nature, or behind nature – but that we
regard what has been revered as "God" not as "divine"
but as wretched, absurd, pernicious; not as an error but as
a *crime against life*. . . . We deny God as God. . . . If the
existence of this Christian God were *proved* to us, we
should feel even less able to believe in Him. . . . A religion
such as Christianity which never once comes into touch
with reality, and which collapses the very moment reality
asserts its rights even on one single point, must naturally
be a mortal enemy of the "wisdom of this world". . . .'
'What meaning', he continues in *Ecce Homo* (another work
of his last period), 'have those lying concepts, those
handmaids of morality, "Soul", "Spirit", "Free Will",
"God", if their aim is not the psychological ruin of
mankind? What earnestness is diverted from the instincts
that aim at self-preservation and an increase of bodily
energy, i.e. at an increase of life, when anaemia is raised to
an ideal and the contempt of the body is construed as the
"salvation of the soul"; what is all this if it is not a recipe
for decadence?'

Only an invalid, afraid of losing the remnants of his
'bodily energy', could have struggled with Nietzsche's fury
against his own religious instinct. Besides, he knew full
well that nothing but a formidable enemy could impel him

to mobilize the stamina required for such a fight. And an enemy of this kind he saw above all in official Christianity which he attacked with religious fervour and fanaticism. His real disposition was not one of irreligion, but of frantic *anti-religion*. This is why now and then he touched – from the other end as it were – on some of the profounder aspects of the very religion he attacked. For instance, in his anti-Christian campaign he even expressed, and repeatedly, his admiration for the personality of Christ, as well as for sincere Christian ascetics. 'All reverence on my part to the ascetic ideal, in so far as it is honourable,' he says in one of his aphorisms, 'so long as it believes in itself and plays no pranks on us! But I like not all these coquettish bugs who have an insatiable ambition to smell of the infinite until eventually the infinite smells of bugs.'

Unconsciously drawn to Christ and to the highest aspects of Christian teaching so well described in *The Anti-Christ*, he was yet anxious to justify his own rebellion against both by certain forms of historical Christianity in which he was unable to see anything but weakness, mendacity and utilitarian cant. 'The fatal feature of Christianity lies in the necessary fact that its faith had become as morbid, base and vulgar as the needs to which it had to administer were base and vulgar', he declared in the same book. But even apart from this, both his logic and his taste rose against the idea of a vengeful God which – in his opinion – was as offensive to religion as it was to common sense, and most of all to one's own sense of decency.

'How he raged at us, this wrath-monster, because we understood him badly! But why did he not speak more clearly! And if the fault lay in our ears, why did he give us ears that heard him badly?

'Too much miscarried with him, this potter who had not learned thoroughly! That he took revenge on his pots and creations, however, because they turned out badly – that was a sin against *good taste*.

'There is also good taste in piety: *this* at last said: "Away with *such* a God! Better to have no God, better to set up

destiny on one's own account, better to be a fool, better to
be God oneself!"'

This kind of rebellious unbelief was itself a proof of
Nietzsche's ineradicable religious instinct. 'O Zarathustra,
thou art more pious than thou believest, with such an
unbelief', the Pope out of Service exclaimed after his talk
with Zarathustra. 'Some God in thee hath converted thee
to thine ungodliness. Is it not thy piety itself which no
longer letteth thee believe in God?'

### 3

'Ungodliness' as expressed by Nietzsche is likely to be
found when men's current idea of God has not progressed
with their mental and moral development: God, or at any
rate a God thus limited, is simply left behind. This is why
one can repudiate theism without at all abrogating one's
religious consciousness. Nietzsche himself pointed this out
in one of his aphorisms: 'Why atheism nowadays? It appears
to me that though the religious instinct is in vigorous
growth – it rejects the theistic satisfaction with profound
distrust.' Besides, only a latent Christian of the highest
order, who is attacking his own secret inclinations, could
have been so violently anti-Christian as Nietzsche was.
This is why his anti-religious fury should not be taken at its
face value, nor its effect be over-exaggerated.* Even his
gospel of hardness was inverted Christian charity – a
virtue of which he wanted to rid himself, but in vain. His
sister tells us that several pious women who were in
contact with him simply refused to believe that he was not
a good Christian. She also relates how during his walks in
the environs of Basle, Nietzsche took a fancy to a sick child
and tended him like a nurse just to make him happy. He
even made arrangements for placing him at his own
expense in an infirmary but, to Nietzsche's sorrow, the

---

* In one of his letters (to H. Albert) Paul Valéry wrote, in
August 1903, about Nietzsche's attacks on Christianity: 'Ses
critiques du Christianisme sont des ombres – brossant l'ombre
d'un Chrétien' ('His criticisms of Christianity are shadows
brushing the shadow of a Christian').

little invalid died meanwhile. This is only one of the many illustrations of Nietzsche's genuine charity. Had he been a real pagan he would certainly have insisted much less on his 'physiological' paganism than he did. And did he not himself confess that in him the Christianity of his forbears, with their 'stern intellectual conscience, fostered by Christianity', had turned against itself in order to go beyond itself?

Whether it entirely succeeded in this is a different matter. The whole of Nietzsche's inner make-up was nearer to a self-tormented Pascal, or even St Paul, than to an ancient Greek. In a letter to Brandes he himself says of Pascal that he is 'almost in love with him, because he has taught me an infinite amount. He is the only logical Christian.' At the same time, the very manner in which Nietzsche tackled the problem puts the dilemma before us all: are we still Christians, or are we not? *Can* we still be sincere Christians at all? And if not, what is the reason? And what is the alternative? Even in the case of genuine believers, Nietzsche demanded that in the name of conscience and spiritual integrity one should test one's Christian faith through its opposites before definitely accepting it. Those who are still Christians at heart 'owe it *to their faith* that they should thus for once take up their abode in the wilderness – if for no other reason than that of being able to pronounce on the question whether Christianity is needful. . . . Your evidence on the question will be valueless until you have lived for years without Christianity, and with the utmost desire to continue to exist without it: until, indeed, you have withdrawn far, far away from it. It is not when your nostalgia urges you back again, but when your judgement, based on a strict comparison, drives you back, that your homecoming has any significance.' (*The Dawn of Day*)

The personal reasons why Nietzsche himself refused a homecoming of this kind have already been pointed out. But as his religious temperament looked for some outlet even on a biological plane, he projected into his Zara-thustra a number of compensations for his own repressed

religiosity – in the form of passionate anti-religion.
Zarathustra is in fact a compendium of such compensations and, for this very reason, an idealized *alter ego* of
Nietzsche himself. There were two substitutes in particular which he had worked out mainly in order to satisfy his
religious instinct: the idea of Dionysus, and that of
'eternal recurrence'.

<h2 style="text-align:center">4</h2>

As has already been pointed out, the first of the two was
defined by Nietzsche (in *The Birth of Tragedy*) not as an
act of transcending one's individual consciousness, but
rather of ecstatically dissolving it in Nature, in the pre-
individual collective consciousness, or even in the universal
Will. 'From the height of joy in which man feels himself
completely and utterly a deified form and self-justification
of nature, down to the joy of healthy peasants and healthy
semi-human beasts, the whole of this long and enormous
gradation of the light and colour of *happiness* was called by
the Greek – not without that grateful quivering of one
who is initiated into the secret, not without much caution
and pious silence – by the god-like name of Dionysus.' In
the Greece of the sixth century BC, the differentiation
between the individual and the collective group-soul was
perhaps not yet finally completed; and so the temptation
to return to the latter – via all sorts of orgiastic Dionysian
rites or festivals – and dissolve in it must have been
strong indeed.

Refusing to become a believer, let alone a mystic on a
Christian plane, Nietzsche the invalid thus philandered
with an ersatz mysticism on the plane of the 'biological'
man, who, instead of transcending nature, returns to her
in a pantheistic sense. Yet the 'Dionysian' outburst of
instincts, separated from or turned against both spirituality
and reasoning, may lead to inner turmoil and chaos,
especially when Apollo – the god of harmony and balance –
is not at hand. As Nietzsche could neither reconcile the
Christian and the 'Dionysian' elements within his
consciousness nor side entirely with Dionysus, the tension

between them only increased. Judging by the letters he sent to a number of people between Christmas 1888 and 8 January 1889, the clash between the two reached, during his mental collapse, such a pitch that he *identified* himself now with Dionysus, now with Christ. The letters addressed to Professor Overbeck and his wife, to Erwin Rohde and to Cosima Wagner, are signed 'Dionysus'. Those he sent to King Umberto, to Mariani (the Vatican Secretary of State), and to the ruling house of Baden bear the signature 'The Crucified One'.

Whatever the causes of Nietzsche's final breakdown, the gap between 'Dionysus' and 'The Crucified One' may even have speeded up that crisis which led to a tragic *dénouement*. Nor was the idea of Eternal Recurrence of much help to him either – not in the long run, although at first it may have looked like a plausible substitute for eternity. Nietzsche, at any rate, took it as such and was even anxious to arrive at a scientific foundation or confirmation of it, without suspecting that in the light of our present-day science Eternal Recurrence would eventually be proclaimed a fallacy. This is what Sir Arthur Eddington says on the subject in his *New Pathways in Science* 'By accepting the theory of the expanding universe, we are relieved of one conclusion which we had felt to be intrinsically absurd. It was argued that every possible configuration of atoms must repeat itself at some distant date. But that was on the assumption that the atoms will have only the same choice of configuration in the future as they have now. In an expanding space any particular congruence becomes more and more improbable. The expansion of the universe creates new possibilities of distribution faster than the atoms can work through them, and there is no longer any likelihood of any particular distribution being repeated.'

Still, regardless of any of its initial promises or disappointments, the idea of 'eternal recurrence' itself soon revealed so much horror for the suffering Nietzsche that he had to summon up a truly supra-human courage in order to face its consequences (the eternal repetitions of his own predicament). This will become clearer, however, if we first mention some of the major problems Nietzsche had to cope with, not least that of God.

5

'The most important fact in recent history – that "God is dead", that belief in the Christian God has become unworthy of professing – is already beginning to cast its first shadow over Europe. To the few, at least, whose suspecting glance is strong enough, and subtle enough for this drama, some sun seems to have set, some old profound confidence seems to have changed into doubt: our old world must seem to them daily more darksome, distrustful, strange and old. In the main, however, one may say that the event itself is far too great, too remote, too much beyond people's power of apprehension, for one to suppose that so much as the report of it could have *reached* them; not to speak of many who already knew what had *really* taken place, and what must all collapse now that this belief has been undermined.'

This passage alone, taken from *The Joyful Wisdom*, is an indication of the seriousness with which Nietzsche judged religion and Christianity. For while proclaiming to the world the 'death' of the Christian God, he realized full well the consequences of such a fact, and above all the gradual but inevitable crumbling away of the entire system of morality which was based on God's existence. Always liable to draw final conclusions, he saw at once that a moral void and anarchy would spread all over the world unless a working alternative was found soon enough. The laments of his 'Madman with the Lamp', on becoming aware of the 'murder' of God, contain some of Nietzsche's own fears and misgivings. 'Whither are we travelling? Away from all suns? Is there still a height and a depth? Are we not wandering towards everlasting annihilation? Do we not perceive the indications of this immense void? Is it not colder? Is not the night becoming darker and darker? Must we not light our lanterns at noon?' (*The Joyful Wisdom*.)

Much of Nietzsche's philosophy was one prolonged attempt to light the lantern in this darkness at noon. The very anxiety with which he set out to do this is a proof of how complicated his attitude towards the problem of God must have seemed to him. IIe was the last person to ignore its seriousness, and was as much tormented by it as was his older contemporary Fyodor Dostoyevsky. Nietzsche went so far indeed as to consider the 'death of God' the central event in mankind's moral history. But this itself imbued his own task with a direction and a dramatic grandeur big enough to stir all his will and aspirations. The task he now saw before him was in fact nothing less than to save the world from that vacuum which threatened to engulf it once God had been ousted – ousted beyond recall – from the consciousness and conscience of man. Aware of the gravity of the dilemma, Nietzsche was all the more tempted to think that he was called upon to overcome it by finding the right alternative. History – so he thought – had ordained that he himself should be a new saviour, pointing the path towards the future destiny of a mankind deprived of God. Hence his frequent references to his own person as being 'fate and fatality'. Yet this only landed him in further inconsistencies and contradictions – which are well worth exploring.

### 6

The mystics speak of a voluntary union between man and God, enabling the individual to achieve his highest self-realization on earth in the name of a meaning or Value which only the highest Being, that is God, can confer upon life through revelation. But the ecstasy of such a mystical union has its negative counterpart in the ecstasy of what might be called magical self-assertion in its two aspects – one of them implying belief in God, and the other utter unbelief. In the first case one repudiates God either because one fails to find the supreme Value in Him, or else because one wants to assert one's freedom from God.* In

* This inner process is tackled in *Dostoyevsky*, by the present author, published by Russell and Russell, New York, 1969.

the case of unbelief, however, one challenges not God but the senselessness of a world deprived of God and hence of any highest Value as well. Having discarded God, the self-assertive individual may even proclaim himself the only divinity. Intoxicated with the temporary illusion of his own demonic power, he measures his daring by the very amount of the void he is able to face and to endure. If in the past he required a God, he now actually 'delights in cosmic disorder without a God, a world of accident, to the essence of which terror, ambiguity and seductiveness belong'.

Certain reckless souls inflate themselves with such spurious power, although they may be crushed by the nihilism it implies. What happens is that the burden of the cosmic vacuum around them grows and finally threatens to become even heavier than a most tyrannical God. Hence Nietzsche's warning in *The Joyful Wisdom*: 'We have left the land and have gone aboard ship! We have broken down the bridges behind us – nay, more, the land behind us! Well, little ship! Look out! Beside thee is the ocean. . . . Times will come when thou wilt feel that it is infinite, and that there is nothing more frightful than infinity. Oh, the poor bird that felt itself free and now strikes against the walls of this cage! Alas, what if homesickness for the land should attack thee, as if there had been more *freedom* there – and there is no land any longer.'

Nietzsche's conclusions are hardly meant to lessen one's homesickness for the land. In this infinity of the void he sees but a casual chaotic universe, without any goal or meaning. And since its process is a blind one, there can be no real difference between crime and virtue, or even between life and death. 'The living is only a species of the dead being, and a very rare species. . . .' Yet Nietzsche with his inverted religious instinct did not falter. His defiance made him plunge into the void with the pride of a self-appointed god. The more so because he was now determined to re-mould the whole of life and to confer upon it at least that illusory man-made significance of which it was still capable in such a state of things. He was to be the great transvaluer imposing a meaning upon a meaningless

world. Was it not his duty to become worthy of such a high
calling? 'God is dead! And we have killed Him! How shall
we be consoled for this, we murderers of murderers? He
whom the world held to be most sacred and most powerful
has bled on our knives – who shall wash the stain of this
blood from us? In what water can we be purified? Is not
the very greatness of this act too great for us? Must not we
ourselves become Gods to seem worthy of it? Never before
was so great a deed performed – and all those born after us
will, by this very fact, belong to a higher form of history
than any that has hitherto existed.' (*The Joyful Wisdom*.)

While reading these lines one cannot help recalling
Dostoyevsky's maniac Kirillov (in *The Possessed*) who,
before Nietzsche and for analogous reasons, divided
history into two parts: from the gorilla to man, and from
man to man-god through the 'death of God'. Having
abolished God altogether, he was *bound* to regard himself
as God and his own demonic selfwill (or will to power) as
divine. But as he was unable to accept or endure his
'divinity' in the senseless and blindly evil universe he was
doomed to live in, he saw that the only 'freedom' left to
him was the freedom to protest against it all and reject it by
committing suicide. The final act of his self-assertion was
self-annihilation. Such was the outcome of his 'new
terrible liberty' – as he called it. The ensuing void *can* yet
apparently be filled at times by the pride of a self-appointed
task of such magnitude as to make one ready to dispense
with God, no matter whether He does or does not exist.
This kind of Satanic consciousness (representing the
negative pole of an essentially religious mind) can be felt
in many a page of Nietzsche's *Thus Spake Zarathustra*.

'God is a conjecture: but I do not wish your conjecturing
to reach beyond your creating will.

'Could ye *conceive* a God? Then, I pray you, be silent
about all Gods! But ye could well create a superman.

'And how would ye endure life without that hope, ye
discerning ones? Neither in the conceivable could ye have
been born, nor in the irrational.

'But that I may reveal my heart entirely unto you, my

friends: If there were Gods, how could I bear to be no God!
Therefore there are no Gods.'

Here, if anywhere, the physical superman merges with
the proud man-god. The very recklessness of his challenge
may allure him as an adventure full of dangerous experi-
ments upon his 'freedom'. The invalid Nietzsche, who saw
in the amount of pain he was able to withstand a proof of
his stoic courage, could not but welcome such a senseless
universe as another test for his own power of endurance.
'We philosophers and "free spirits" feel ourselves irradi-
ated, as by a new, rosy dawn, by the report that the "old
God is dead"; our hearts thereby overflow with gratitude,
astonishment, presentiment, and expectation. At last the
horizon seems once more unobstructed, granting even that
it is not bright: our ships can at last start on their voyage
once more, in face of every danger: every risk is again per-
mitted to the knowing ones; the sea, our sea, again lies
open before us; perhaps there was never such an open sea.

This drug-like exultation, which he now required in
stronger and stronger doses, marked his process of
demonic self-assertion as distinct from true self-realization.
Yet having escaped from the 'tyranny' of God, such an
adventurous man-god is landed, sooner or later, in another
and worse tyranny – the determinism of a blind mechanistic
universe. For if we are but casual biological bubbles in a
process of equally casual cosmic forces, then our consciousness as well as our volition, with all its acts, is determined
down to its minutest details not by us, but by those forces,
or the immutable laws of Nature – call them what you will.

But is not then Nietzsche's concept of 'man-god's
tyrannical will' as illusory as the values it rejects? The
titanic man-god thus reaches an impasse fraught with
dangers which Nietzsche could not have avoided. On the
other hand, the passion with which he defied the idea of
God betrayed his repressed longing for him. One cannot
but recall the religious poem he wrote at Pforta in 1864:
'Once more, before my vision turns . . .' An equally
religious but less defiant temperament would have
satisfied this longing by bowing to God; but in Nietzsche's

case an issue of this sort was out of the question: in the
state of health he was in, such a line of least resistance
would have been a proof of his own weakness and resignation.

### 7

Like Dostoyevsky's Ivan Karamazov, Nietzsche repudiated God with the greater vehemence the more he was
secretly longing for Him. The two cases were analogous, but not identical. Ivan rebelled because of other
people's sufferings, whereas Nietzsche was concerned
primarily with the suffering he himself had to face. In fact,
hopeless invalid as he was, he might have been tempted to
look to God for the last solace and comfort, provided he
was willing to resign himself and submit to divine Providence. But Nietzsche chose the path of rebellion. His
pride would not allow him to 'wag his tail' before God,
especially when he knew that he needed Him as a shelter.

It was here that the magnitude of his suffering became,
once again, a measure of his defiance, while the defiance
itself kept intensifying his imagined or wishful greatness
and power. Besides, if Nietzsche had suddenly embraced a
faith in God, then his own exceptional mission would have
become superfluous – the mission designed for a godless
world. For he, Nietzsche, was destined to open the eyes of
humanity, to warn it of all the dangers ahead, and, what
was more, to show the only possible way to a future devoid
of God. It was unthinkable for him to part with such a
mission, which had become the very pivot of his own life.

But Nietzsche's unconscious longing for God remained.
One of the many proofs to this effect is the lament poured
out by the Magician in Zarathustra's cave. The lament,
expressed in the form of a highly agitated poem, is too long
to be quoted in full; but a glance at the text is enough to
reveal a lonely 'God-tormented' mind who curses and at
the same time invokes God with all the passion of a repressed religious temperament. Although referring –
supposedly – to the 'Magician' Richard Wagner, the
lament could be applied to Nietzsche himself whose inner

kinship with his one-time friend he had acknowledged
on several occasions. The ailments and tortures described
in the opening passages in particular are a poetic trans-
position of Nietzsche's own condition, at least during
the worst periods of his illness when, instead of 'wagging
his tail', he preferred to challenge, to blaspheme.

> – Thus do I lie,
> Bend myself, twist myself, convulsed
> With all eternal torture, and smitten
> By thee, cruellest huntsman,
> Thou unfamiliar – God . . .
>
> Smite deeper!
> Smite yet once more!
> Pierce through and rend my heart!
> What meaneth this torture
> With dull indented arrows?
>
> Why look'st thou hither,
> Of human pain not weary,
> With mischief-loving, godly flash-glances?
> Not murder wilt thou,
> But torture, torture?
> For why me torture,
> Thou mischief-loving, unfamiliar God? –

Deserted by humans and by God, he finds his isolation less
endurable than his pain. He is tempted to invoke even the
company of God in order not to feel so lonely in his
affliction.

> Away!
> There fled he surely,
> My final, only comrade,
> My greatest foe,
> Mine unfamiliar –
> My hangman – God . . .
>
> – Nay!
> Come thou back!
> *With* all thy great tortures!

To me the last of lonesome ones,
Oh, come thou back!
All my hot tears in streamlets trickle
Their course to thee!
Oh, come thou back
Mine unfamiliar God!
My pain!
My final bliss!

# 5 The superman

After his breach with Lou and Rée, Nietzsche must have felt even more of a lonely refugee than usual. In his quest for a place where he could find some rest and relief from his troubles he settled for the winter of 1882-3 at Rapallo. During his walks in the environs of this Mediterranean town the idea of the nobler human type he had been dreaming of became so clear in his mind that it crystallized in the symbolic and prophetic figure of his Zarathustra. The inspiration was so powerful that when he sat down to put his vision on to paper he finished the whole of the first part of *Thus Spake Zarathustra* in about ten days. By the middle of February 1883 the manuscript, with its twenty-two talks (*Reden*), was ready for print; but when it was published it found hardly any buyers or readers. Its message and its literary excellence were evidently wasted on Nietzsche's contemporaries.

The summer of 1883 was spent by him in Engadine. Here he wrote the second part of his masterpiece. This time, too, it did not take him longer than ten days to complete it. The third part was written by him at Nice during January and February 1884, while the fourth (and last) part he finished at Menton by the middle of the following February. When in the spring of 1884 the second and third parts appeared in print together, the response was again so negligible that after their failure Nietzsche could find no publisher for the fourth part of this work. So he issued it at his own expense in forty copies only, to be distributed among his friends and acquaintances.

The subtitle of *Thus Spake Zarathustra* was 'A Book for All and for No One'. In practice it proved to be for no one, since there were hardly any buyers. And this despite the fact (or perhaps because of it) that it was Nietzsche's greatest achievement: a book of condensed wisdom in which philosophy passes into poetry and poetry into

philosophy. All this in addition to his wonderful rhythmical
language with its striking similes interspersed with
devastating ironical outbursts. Zarathustra himself is the
archetype of the Wise Old Man and also the prophet even
in the traditional biblical sense, however secular and anti-
religious his gospel of a new saviour, the superman, may
be.

When Zarathustra, laden with wisdom, leaves his lonely
mountain cave and goes to human beings with the message
that 'man is something that should be overcome' ('der
Mensch ist Etwas, das überwunden werden muss'), he
– like Nietzsche himself – finds no understanding. So he
gathers a small group of disciples and followers. Before
long, however, he returns to his mountain retreat, for he is
anxious that, during his absence, his disciples should now
be able to find and follow themselves. In his renewed
loneliness Zarathustra meditates about the horror of
'eternal recurrence' involving throughout aeons incessant
returns of the same vulgar small men. But now he feels
strong enough to be able to accept life even with such a
prospect.

In the fourth part Zarathustra's lonely cave is visited by
a number of 'higher men'. Among these are two kings
with their donkey ('two kings and only one ass'), an ex-
pope, a soothsayer, a meticulous scientist, and a de-
formed cripple fleeing from human compassion.
Zarathustra, accompanied by his two animals – the proud
eagle and the prudent serpent – welcomes them all. After
his talk about the 'higher man' he treats them to a supper
and, while he takes a temporary leave of them, there
follows an ass festival in the shape of a hilarious parody
upon the old Christian God who is 'dead'. On his return
Zarathustra joins in the happy laughter. Through joy and
laughter he is also anxious to affirm our earthly life despite
its woes; the more so because 'all joy craves for eternity –
craves for profound, profound eternity' ('Doch alle Lust
will Ewigkeit – will tiefe, tiefe Ewigkeit'). Surrounded by
'higher men', he realizes that they are not those whom he
expects; yet he is sure that they too are on their way. It is

his 'great midday', the midday pregnant with the coming superman.

Nietzsche's intention was to continue this work and conclude it with Zarathustra's death, but because of its lack of success he had to give it up. On the other hand, he proceeded to elaborate and comment upon most of its basic ideas in such books as *Beyond Good and Evil* (*Jenseits von Gut und Boese*, 1885), *Genealogy of Morals* (*Die Genealogie der Moral*, 1887), *The Twilight of the Idols* (*Die Götzendämmerung*, 1888), *The Anti-Christ* (1888). The same applies to the notes which were written by Nietzsche between 1883 and 1888, but collected and somewhat arbitrarily 'edited' by his sister Elisabeth under the title of *The Will to Power* (*Der Wille zur Macht*, published in one volume in 1901, and in two volumes in 1906). As for *Thus Spake Zarathustra,* it was recognized as a work of genius only in the 1890s, when (after his mental collapse) Nietzsche's fame suddenly began to spread all over Europe. The first edition containing all four parts appeared in 1892. Five years later it was already in its ninth German edition.

Such was the fate of one of the great books of the last century – a book which can be discussed and written about without end, no matter whether one agrees with it or not. For our purpose it might be sufficient to tackle a few of those points which are likely to throw some further light upon its author's thought, life and fate.

2

One of the salient features in *Thus Spake Zarathustra* is that severe discipline by means of which Nietzsche himself fought for and on behalf of the body. Spurred on by his will to health and by the science of the day, he suppressed in himself without mercy all such inclinations as might have hampered him in this effort. His defence of life thus became also a defence of the body against any encroachments on the part of the 'soul', of traditional morals, and of the world 'beyond'.

'But the awakened one, the knowing one saith: "Body

am I entirely, and nothing more; and soul is only the name of something in the body!"

'The sick and perishing – it was they who despised the body and the earth, and invented the heavenly world, and the redeeming blood-drops: but even those sweet sad poisons they borrowed from the body and the earth!

'From their misery they sought escape, and the stars were too remote for them. Then they sighed: "Oh that there were heavenly paths by which to steal into another existence and into happiness!" Then they contrived for themselves their by-paths and bloody draughts!

'Beyond the sphere of their body and this earth they now fancied themselves transported, these ungrateful ones. But to what did they owe the convulsions and raptures of their transport? To their body and this earth.'

The above passage may provide a clue to Nietzsche's choice of Zarathustra as a destroyer of the old morality in the name of new, entirely different values. The prophet Zarathustra (or Zoroaster) had once founded a religion in which morality was a metaphysical phenomenon and an end in itself. But Nietzsche, who rejected the idea of any metaphysical morals, conjured up Zarathustra in order to make him correct the mistake Zoroaster had made when founding the religion of Zendavesta. That was why he now wanted Zarathustra to raise his voice not on behalf of any metaphysics, but on behalf of earth, the body, and most of all the superman. The name itself was probably taken by him from Goethe. Its physiological implication, on the other hand, Nietzsche derived largely from the Darwinism which was so much in vogue at the time. If, with Darwin's blessing, man has descended from the ape, then why should he not be followed by a still higher species in the same manner as the ape has been followed by man? The conclusion was logical. But Darwin's idea was modified by Nietzsche and in a way corrected by him through that doctrine of the will to power which became the very basis of Nietzschean transvaluation of all values. According to him the essence of life is not the struggle for existence, but the struggle for power, for self-assertion through an accumulation of power. Our consciousness is but a tool in this process. Yet power at its best should not be divorced from what is noble. It should become the very expression of man's nobility.

Viewed from this angle, all that comes from strength and at the same time elevates life is good; all that comes from weakness and the negation of life is bad. The first prerequisite, therefore, is to be strong enough not to succumb in the general struggle for survival, in which (as Nietzsche bluntly puts it) conquest and hardness belong to the very nature of the living being. And they are a consequence of the intrinsic will to power. Equipped with such a notion of the Darwinian survival of the fittest, together with his old idea of the philosopher as teacher and law-giver of mankind, Nietzsche now came definitely forward as prophet of the superman.

3

The idea of the superman, as presented in *Thus Spake Zarathustra,* combined for a while Nietzsche's divergent or even mutually hostile impulses in one powerful focus. The evolutionary biologist exults here side by side with the romantic dreamer and hidden physician. Nietzsche the poet collaborates with Nietzsche the anti-Christian moralist and thinker. The merciless destroyer and breaker of all traditional values works hand in hand with the stern lawgiver; while the laughing Dionysian dancer seems to be on the best of terms with the solemn prophet. Nietzsche's aesthetic, didactic, religious and eugenic propensities thus meet in this book.

*Thus Spake Zarathustra* is a great moral or ethical masterpiece upon an anti-religious plane, destroying all conventional creeds and conventional ethics. Every vital religion chooses for its symbol an ideal Man whose image serves as 'glad tidings' and a way of life for those willing to follow it. Christ and Buddha are obvious examples of such symbols. But there may be other types and ideals of perfection. Among the moderns, Nietzsche alone dared to set up such an ideal on a big scale. Yet prompted largely by his personal needs, this ideal, instead of transcending biology, on the contrary, urged him to reduce everything to a plane which ultimately endangered his own higher objectives. For however lofty one's aspirations, the physical yet cannot escape from the animal. Nietzsche's masterpiece certainly embodies the highest aspirations still possible on the physical plane ennobled by a sincere concern about the fate of man and mankind. And this at a time when he was trying more than ever to find an antidote against nihilist 'decadence' and affirm what he called the 'ascending' type of life. He furthermore identified nihilism with pessimism, the chief source of which was, according to him, physical exhaustion. The only remedy he saw was to combine bodily fitness with a strong and purposefully directed will. In his endeavour to set up a table of values based on this 'new' orientation, he was anxious to point out first of all the fundamental difference between his own theory of 'will to power' and Schopenhauer's blind 'will to exist' which, as we know, had once provided Nietzsche with the very impulse to become a philosopher.

'He certainly did not hit the truth who shot at it the formula: "will to existence": that will doth not exist!

'For what is not, cannot will: that, however, which is in existence – how could it still strive for existence!

'Only where there is life is there also will: not, however, will to life but – so I teach thee – will to power!'

Yet Nietzsche does not make it clear whether such 'will to power' operates as an independent agent, or as a pre-determined tool of 'necessity', or else as a kind of Berg-sonian *élan vital*. He often gives the impression of wavering between these three attitudes, favouring now one, then another – to the confusion of an unprepared reader. What he demanded unconditionally, though, was an abundance of vitality and a will aimed at the highest and at the same time hardest goal attainable on that plane where there is no room for Christian or any other notions of meekness and pity. He made this point clear enough, clearer than any other aspect of his teaching.

'That movement which attempted to introduce itself in a scientific manner on the shoulders of Schopenhauer's morality of pity – a very sad attempt! – is in essence the movement of decadence in morality. Strong ages and noble cultures see something contemptible in pity, in the "love of one's neighbour", and in a lack of egotism and self-esteem.' Nietzsche the invalid knew only too well how much he needed this kind of teaching. The more so because he was also aware of his secret need of loving care, or even of that Christian sympathy and compassion which he rejected wholesale, however, because he saw in them something hostile not only to one's self-esteem, but to life itself. Hence he could not help praising those ages which were more 'positive' in their evaluation of life. To state it in his words, 'ages should be measured according to their *positive force*; valued by this standard, that prodigal and fateful age of the Renaissance appears as the last *great* age, while we moderns, with all our anxious care of ourselves and love of our neighbours, with all our unassuming virtues of industry, equity, and scientific method – with our lust for collection, for economy and for mechanization – represent a weak age.'

Here, if anywhere, one can see the intricate workings of Nietzsche's biological outlook, his *Weltanschauung*. It was under its spell that he revelled in detecting the symptoms of decadence in all the aspects of contemporary life, especially in that Christian-democratic 'herd morality' (as he called it) which, in his opinion, was but a tendency to protect the quantity of the species man at the expense of its quality. In such attempts to undermine the biological excellence of man, he saw cunningly organized weakness, which he regarded as the most blatant expression of the life-denying instinct, parading as a virtue or even as a moral imperative. Already in *The Joyful Wisdom* he had come to the conclusion that our modern European 'disguises himself in morality because he has become a sick, sickly and crippled animal, who has good reasons for being "tame", because he is almost an abortion, an imperfect, weak and clumsy thing. It is not the fierceness of the beast of prey that finds moral disguise necessary, but the gregarious animal, with its profound mediocrity, anxiety and ennui.' From such sophisticated half-truths, it is not difficult to see why Nietzsche was anxious to set up as his ideals even such unscrupulous, robust Renaissance figures as Cesare Borgia. He even went on to assert that all our current morality is 'a sort of counter-movement opposing Nature's endeavours to arrive at a *higher type*. Its effects are: mistrust of life in general (in so far as its tendencies are felt to be immoral); hostility towards the senses (in so much as the highest values are felt to be opposed to the higher instincts); degeneration and self-destruction of "higher natures", because it is precisely in them that the conflict becomes conscious.'

4

As a contrast to all 'taming' morals, whether Christian or otherwise, Nietzsche devised his own rigorous system for rearing an *élite* of humanity. His aim was to mobilize all those instincts which could lead, as he thought, to a stronger species of man. He did not shrink from the implication that mere physical excellence of this kind may often be dangerously near the notorious 'blond beast' – even in its unsublimated shape. But he himself was doing what he could to avoid arriving at such a conclusion by introducing into his 'eugenic' system further principles. These sounded plausible enough, but raised their own queries and were not without pitfalls. For one thing, if the mere amount of physical strength and power is to be the measure of one's right to live and rule, one is still entitled to ask whether there is any guarantee that this power is bound to take the direction of an ascending way of life. It is true that Nietzsche was anxious to combine power only with nobility of character; but what is noble for A may not be noble for B. Power *qua* power has, moreover, the unpleasant propensity of running amok. Who will stop an aggressive barbarian from misusing his power for his own purposes and proclaiming 'noble' only what serves his own interests? Recent history has seen a number of such usurpers, and it will take generations to clear away the ills wrought by them all over the world. The dividing-line between power and brutality is hard to define – and as soon as the difference is gone, the jungle is ushered in again with all its blessings.

Anxious to rear not 'good' but powerful men, Nietzsche thought in terms of the inner and outer tension between all sorts of antitheses. One of his tenets was that 'with every degree of man's growth towards greatness and lofti-ness, he also grows downwards into the depth and into the terrible; we should not desire the one without the other.' As a contrast to the gradual softening of modern Europeans, he thus found it desirable that some sort of 'Promethean barbarians' should force their way into our present-day civilization, 'barbarians coming from above and not from below – thoroughly conquering and ruling natures in search of the material they could mould'. But would not such an *élite* be easily tempted to look upon the rest of mankind, upon the 'many-too-many', as their slaves and treat them accordingly?

Building on these premises, Nietzsche came to the conclusion (largely under the ancient Greek influence, especially that of the poet and aristocrat Theognis) that there were born masters and born slaves. So he postulated an aristocratic class whose fundamental belief ought to be that 'society is *not* allowed to exist for its own sake, but only as a foundation and a scaffolding by means of which a select class of beings may be able to elevate themselves to their highest duties, and in general to a high *existence*.' For this reason he demanded that there should be two opposite sets of values: the ascending one for the ruling masters, and the descending one of the ruled 'herd'. Such was, according to him, the basic division between human beings – a division ordained by Nature herself. But having once adopted this view, Nietzsche was quite willing to put up with the herd-morality, provided the latter was con-fined to the 'herd' only. He even found such a state of things desirable in so far as it procured for the masters material on which they could exercise – as on their own opposites – the creative will to power. While honestly struggling against decadence, he thus toyed with the idea that a process of decay among the masses was not only desirable but even necessary – as a kind of manure required for the growth of a 'higher' *élite*.

It was on this questionable basis that he did his best to revise and reverse the values of Christianity, of democracy and of humanism in general. He did not shrink from recommending the severest methods, provided these would foster the noble supra-human ideal of his choice. Oblivious of the fact that on a mere physiological plane the strict dividing line between supra-human and sub-human is often likely to disappear, Nietzsche could not help occasionally confusing or even blending the two. He objected to the socialists, for example, who believed that circumstances and social combinations could be devised which would put an end to all vice, illness, prostitution and poverty. According to him, the abolition of these evils was neither possible nor even desirable, since they have belonged and will belong to all periods of human history. Where there is growth there must also be refuse and decaying matter, for such is the law of vital processes. The highest culture and the most abject corruption and decay are parallel phenomena. They are necessary to each other. Perhaps they even condition each other.

Along this path of reasoning Nietzsche was logically compelled to advocate the co-existence of antithetic 'ascending' and 'descending' values, regulated by the principle of hierarchy or, as he put it, by the order of rank. 'My philosophy aims at a new *order of rank*,' he says in *The Will to Power*: '*not* an individualist morality. The spirit of the herd should rule within the herd – but not beyond it: the leaders of the herd require a fundamentally differ-ent valuation for their actions, as do also the independent ones or the beasts of prey.' Such words as the 'beast of prey' may sound shocking, but Nietzsche used them also as a contrast to the gentle and therefore 'decadent' features he had found in his own nature. Since he thoroughly disapproved of all that was meek, gentle and Christian in himself, he championed with all the greater fervour a more robust and healthier breed of humanity, worthy of the future.

And the standard of values? It was again one of biological fitness and power. 'The modicum of power which you represent decides your rank: all the rest is cowardice.' But such a reply may remind one of a Prussian general mustering his forces for a battle. Carried away by his own theory of hierarchy and power, Nietzsche never tired of repeating, in his habitual sweeping manner, that great cultures have sprung up, so far, only in those communities which were founded on exploitation or even on slavery. He nevertheless made concessions and seemed to vacillate between the principle of exploitation and that of co-operation. There were moments when he was inclined to reconcile the two. Moreover, in his anti-democratic campaign he began to look upon hardship and suffering as a privilege reserved for the pioneers of the 'ascending' life. As for the 'good' masses, they should be spared the trials of the elect. Make them contented and happy by all means, but on one condition: that they should keep their decayed and decaying 'Christian' morality only to themselves, thereby upholding the order of rank. 'I have declared war,' he says, 'on the anaemic Christian ideal (together with what is closely related to it), but only to put an end to its tyranny and clear the way for other *ideals*, for more robust ideals. . . .' Yet he adds that the continuance of Christian ideals as such 'belongs to the most desirable of desiderata; if only for the sake of the ideals which wish to take their stand beside it and perhaps above it – they must have opponents, and strong ones, too – in order to grow strong themselves. . . . The necessity of *creating gulfs*, distance, and the order of rank, is therefore imperative; but not the necessity of retarding the process mentioned above.'

## 5

Considering himself a physician of his own ailments as well as of those of mankind, Nietzsche magnified the task

undertaken by him to a degree where his personal suffering became inseparable from the great role he thought he
was called upon to play. There were moments when he
was ready to welcome any increase of his own malady
simply in order to prove thereby worthy of his role and
grow stronger through his growing resistance. He who
wants to cure, to lead and to rule others, must first prove
that he is fit for such a task, and he can do this only through
victories over himself.

'The terrible task of a ruler who educates himself: the
kind of man and people over which he will rule must be
forecast in him: it is in himself, therefore, that he must
become a ruler.

'The great educator, like nature, must elevate obstacles
in order that these may be overcome.'

His personal predicament was thus best justified in his
own eyes by an over-personal goal of titanic dimensions.
He needed a goal which would raise his own tragedy to a
height lofty enough to bolster up his vitality, his pride and
his defiance. This is what he wrote to his sister Elisabeth
in August 1883: 'The whole meaning of the terrible
suffering to which I was exposed lies in the fact that I was
torn away from an estimate of my life-task which was not
only false but a hundred times *too low*. And since by
nature I belong to the most modest of men, some violent
means was necessary to recall me to myself.' His new life-
task was adequately summed up in *Thus Spake Zarathustra*. But even here Nietzsche had to contend with
inconsistencies, since his strategy in defence of life would
often leave him no other choice. Even some of those basic
positions of his to which he clung with such tenacity, can
hardly disguise their illusory nature. Which brings us
again to his doctrine of the 'eternal recurrence', as well as
to his belief in what he called 'amor fati' ('love of one's
fate') – in this case his own.

The two should actually be explored together, since in
Nietzsche's case they are complementary and represent
the two aspects of one and the same blind alley. We have
already seen how important – psychologically important –

was the element of resistance in Nietzsche's struggle.
Determined to prove his own right to live, he exercised his
will and his endurance to their uttermost. But in his state
of health he could do so mainly through a resistance to the
worst possibilities that fate continued to inflict upon him.
Not to flinch before anything became one of his slogans –
more, one of his methods. Hence the desperate character
of his stoicism which in its very defiance contained even a
love of pain and adversity. He actually welcomed these in
so far as they gave him a pretext for affirming life when he
was most tempted to say 'No' to it. There came however
the crucial moment when he was logically compelled to
face the meaninglessness of life and the universe with the
composure of a man who would not shrink from the most
horrible conclusions imaginable; a moment in fact which
threatened to reduce even his dogma of the will to power to
a mere illusion. After all, if life and the universe are
nothing more than an interplay of blind forces, then man's
ego, man's will and consciousness, are only part and parcel
of these forces, foreordained by the immutable laws of
nature in such a manner as to leave no room for any free
action or free volition whatever. All happens because it
must happen. All is determined not by us but by the
mechanical world process. In this case Nietzsche himself
was – like everybody else – but a little cog in the blind
universal clockwork, and all his grandiloquent talk about
the superman destined to alter the very course of mankind's
history sounded like mockery. Nietzsche the invalid saw
this formidable trap, and made at once the strategic
*volte-face* required. Heedless of logical or any other
contradictions, he hurried to 'transvalue' the rigid 'thou
must', imposed by the blind cosmic mechanism, into the
would-be free and would-be heroic 'I myself willed it so.'

'As a composer, riddle-reader, and redeemer of chance,'
says Zarathustra, 'did I teach them to create the future,
and all that hath been – to redeem by creating.

'The past of man to redeem, and every "it was" to
transform until the Will said: But so did I will it. So shall
I will it –

'This did I call redemption: this alone did I call redemption.'

Yet no matter what labels Zarathustra may have given it, the inexorable 'thou must' of the world-machine could by no means really be turned into the freedom of 'I willed it so'. The deadlock was complete, and no strategic or tactical ruse was able to alter it. Hence Nietzsche's private uncertainty, so different from his high-sounding words in public. In a letter to Erwin Rohde, written in May 1887, he referred to Jacob Burckhardt, Hippolyte Taine and himself as the three fundamental nihilists 'irrevocably bound to one another', and concluded: 'As you perhaps suspect, I have not yet abandoned all hope of finding a way out of the abyss by means of which we can arrive at something.' This avowal was made by him at a time when his idea of being a supposed leader and law-giver of mankind had already reached its climax. Torn between an anti-religious that is, spirit-denying, view of man's existence on the one hand, and his repressed religiosity on the other, he had finally reached a position from which he could neither go forward nor turn back. It was here that he performed a logical and psychological *tour de force* by insisting upon his expedient of 'amor fati'.

## 6

The change of the fatalistic 'thou must' into the would-be free 'I willed it so' was a move by means of which Nietzsche hoped not only to rescue one of the fundamental tenets of his philosophy, but also to say 'Yes' to life even when he knew that mechanical 'eternal recurrence' would imply – in his own case – nothing less than countless repetitions of the same excruciating pain and suffering he had to bear in this existence. Again and again they would be inflicted upon him throughout eternity. Was not such a prospect too terrifying for anybody's power of endurance?

In *The Joyful Wisdom* the invalid Nietzsche formulated the dilemma from his own personal standpoint: 'What if a demon crept after thee into thy loneliest loneliness some day or night and said to thee, "This life, as thou livest it at

present, and hast lived it, thou must live once more, and
also innumerable times; and there will be nothing new in
it, but every pain, and every joy, and every thought, and
every sigh, and all the unspeakably small and great things
in thy life must come to thee again, and all in the same
series and sequences – and similarly this spider and this
moonlight among the trees, and similarly this moment,
and I myself. The eternal hour-glass of existence will ever
be turned once more, and thou with it, thou speck of
dust." Wouldst thou not throw thyself down and gnash
thy teeth, and curse the demon that so spake?' But had
Nietzsche himself done such a thing, he would have
acknowledged thereby his own defeat. Unable to give up
his proud 'I willed it so', he had recourse, once again, to
his 'artifice of self-preservation' in order to convince
himself that the choice between accepting or rejecting
existence on these terms was still his – in so far as he
'freely' said 'Yes' to the inevitable. And so the above
passage from *The Joyful Wisdom* was completed in these
words: 'The question touching all and everything, "Dost
thou want this once more and also innumerable times?"
would lie as the heaviest burden upon thy activity! Or,
how wouldst thou have to become favourably inclined
to thyself and to life, so as *to long for nothing more ardently*
than for this last eternal sanctioning and sealing?'

Anxious as he was to remain 'favourably inclined' to
himself and to life, Nietzsche answered with precisely this
kind of sanctioning and sealing. Two delusions – the
'amor fati' and the 'eternal recurrence' – thus met and
blended in order to enable him to accept and affirm his own
life even in its most terrifying shape. Yet the necessity of
the cosmic clockwork cannot be transmuted into individual
freedom – it can only be faked into a semblance of such
freedom, and the awareness of this fact is enough to bring
one to a final negation of life. Among Nietzsche's posthumous writings there actually is a passage under the title,
'The Innocence of Becoming', in which one can read this
startling confession: 'I do not want to live *again*. How was
I able to withstand life? Through having been a creator.

What was it that made it possible for me to endure looking into the future [*Ausblick*]? The vision of the superman who says *Yea* to existence. I myself tried to say *Yea* to it – alas!'

A retreat from such an impasse towards a conscious religious attitude was, at this date, no longer possible for Nietzsche, since it would have meant a refutation of his 'message' and his entire lifework as a creator. The only thing to do was to entrench himself behind yet another *volte-face*. So he cast his skin again and adopted once more the aesthetic illusion even in Schopenhauer's sense and in that of his own *Birth of Tragedy*. If truth becomes terrifying past endurance, there always remains a refuge, a respite, offered by one's aesthetic illusion, by the 'metaphysical comfort' of art, and why indeed not take it?

'Art and nothing else!' he exclaimed in *The Will to Power*, when commenting on his first book. 'Art is the great means of making life possible, the great seducer of life, the great stimulus to life.

'Art is the alleviation of the seeker after knowledge – of him who recognizes the terrible and questionable character of existence, and who *desires* to recognize it – of the tragic seeker after knowledge.

'Art is the alleviation of the man of action – of him who not only sees the terrible and questionable character of existence, but also lives it, desires to live it – of the tragic and warlike man, the hero.

'Art is the alleviation of the sufferer – as the way to states in which pain is willed, is transfigured, is deified, where suffering is a form of great ecstasy.'

At the end of his career, Nietzsche was thus even nearer to the vacuum and the futility of existence than at the beginning. And, strangely enough, he himself came back to his own starting-point. Both *The Birth of Tragedy* and *The Will to Power* agree that 'art is more valuable than truth'. Such an attitude helped him to barricade himself at least against the most destructive consequences of his own *Weltanschauung*. What is more, it gave him a promise to transmute his personal suffering into a 'form of great ecstasy', and this was perhaps the main thing as far as he was concerned.

## 7

What all such philosophizing with clenched teeth must have cost him can be gathered from his own hint in a letter to Professor Overbeck (July 1885) where we come across the following sentence: 'My life consists at present in the wish that all things be *different* from the manner in which I understand them, and that someone would discredit my "truths" in my own eyes [und dass mir jemand meine "Wahrheiten" unglaubwürdig mache].'

One of the reasons why he stuck to his position to the bitter end, was his determination not to give way to weakness or to defeat – the most unpardonable sin against life in a sufferer. But was not the 'metaphysical comfort' of art he now adopted once more also a sign of defeat? And so may have been the very 'strength' with which he persevered in his state of warfare against himself. By refusing a spiritual or religious solution he abandoned perhaps the only path which might have led him to an integration of his split personality, especially if we assume that what is called the spiritual plane is the complement rather than the antithesis of the physical plane. Supposing even that our spirit is (in Nietzsche's words) 'only the name of something in the body', we still cannot dismiss the fact that this 'something' has a life of its own which refuses to be forced back to mere physiology.* A narrow physiological view might in fact be as harmful to an 'ascending' type of life as the one-sided spirituality of the ascetics. It might preclude even a successful physiological existence. If, as Nietzsche contends, truth is but that kind of error without which certain species of humanity cannot exist, then why should we refuse to adopt that religious attitude which promises an integrated life here on earth, and a deeper and fuller life than mere physiology could ever

---

* Among recent psychologists it was Carl Jung in particular who rejected the idea that man's spiritual life is only a superstructure upon his 'instinctual life'.

give us? In the worst case this would only be one 'vital error' set up against another and less vital one.

The very violence of his anti-religious campaign was a proof that he must have been attacking the Christian propensities he felt in himself and wanted to get rid of. Precisely because Nietzsche the invalid knew all the allurements of Christian faith, he intensified his defiance, until his hatred of Christian moral values in particular knew no limits. 'As long as your morality hung over me, I breathed like one asphyxiated', he exclaimed 'That is why I throttled the snake. I wished to live, consequently it had to die.' Yet in so far as he freed himself from Christian morals, he did not do this in order to indulge in immorality. On the contrary, his own standard of moral values demanded a discipline the strictness of which would have frightened away the majority of so-called Christians. Having confined himself to his body, Nietzsche discarded everything connected with the soul and spirit in a trans-cendental sense. But in doing so he was quite willing to praise that inner earnestness which once upon a time helped to fashion the European Christian ideal. In his opinion, 'morality *itself* in the form of honesty urges us to reject those morals, in the transcendental premises of which we no longer believe and, indeed, cannot believe'.*

Whatever his purely personal reasons, it was above all Nietzsche's own inherited moral sense, the sense of honesty, that turned against a morality which – with the 'death of God' – he considered obsolete. So he was the more anxious to set up such a moral code as might best serve life in its earthly sense. Assuming that no actions are moral in themselves but can only become so in our interpretation of them, he felt entitled to interpret the whole of life in the light of those vitalist principles which he regarded as fully acceptable to the new anti-religious consciousness. Hence the ruthlessness of his transvalua-tions, the first victim of which was to be the entire system of our old Christian values. In this respect he certainly went 'beyond good and evil', but only in order to create

* *The Will to Power.*

new values of good and evil for the sake of a higher kind of life and of man here on earth. This is why his moral rules often resemble a severe yoga-system (devised for the training of supermen) and can in fact be defined as puritanism viewed from the opposite pole.

Even in his last phase he thoroughly appreciated the disciplining role of Christian morals at their best, as we can conclude from the following passage in *The Will to Power*: 'To what extent is the self-destruction of morality still a sign of its own strength? We Europeans have taken within us the blood of those who were ready to die for their faith; we have taken morality terribly seriously, and there is nothing which we have not, at one time or other, sacrificed to it. On the other hand, our intellectual subtlety has been reached essentially through the vivisection of our conscience. We do not yet know the "whither" towards which we are urging our steps, now that we have departed from the soil of our forbears. But it was on this very soil that we acquired the strength which is now driving us from our homes in search of adventure, and it is thanks to that strength that we are now in mid-sea, surrounded by untried possibilities and things discovered – we can no longer choose, we must be conquerors, now that we have no land in which to feel at home and in which we would fain "survive". A concealed "Yea" is driving us forward, and it is stronger than our "Nay". Even our strength no longer bears with us in the old swampy land: we venture into the open, we attempt the task. The world is still rich and undiscovered, and even to perish were better than to be half-men or poisonous men. Our very strength urges us to take to the sea; there where all suns have hitherto sunk we know of a new world.'

## 8

In the 'new world' offered by Nietzsche a maximum of vitality and of physical excellence was to be ennobled by the highest aesthetic heroic ideal he could conceive under the circumstances. His own personal conditions were such as to direct his will and vision towards the most dazzling

contrast to himself; for he knew only too well how much
he needed all sorts of theoretical compensations for the
much too realistic ailments he had to put up with. At the
same time the contrast itself was something more than
just a compensation: it provided him with a disciplining
ideal for himself and for the world at large. Nietzsche was
fully aware of the fact that all morality invented by man is
bound to be relative and therefore might harbour the
motto of 'all things are lawful' in its destructive sense. But
he tried to cope with the dilemma (as far as possible) by
setting up the high standard held by Zarathustra as something obligatory for all those who still care for what
Nietzsche himself assumed to be the ascending type of life.
This however is of little help, since each man can have his
own idea as to what exactly such a type of life means,
without accepting Nietzsche's standard as being absolute
or infallible. The dangerous formula of 'all things are
lawful' is thus by no means eliminated: it lurks behind the
very back of the superman. What else could Nietzsche do
in the end but demand that the formula of 'beyond good
and evil' should become a privilege conferred upon those
only who are big and noble enough not to abuse it? In
order to possess a virtue one must first have the right to it –
that is, one must be made of truly proud and noble
material. Such a man ennobles whatever he takes on. A
man made of ignoble material, on the other hand, has no
right even to be virtuous, since any virtue adopted by him
turns into its own parody or into downright vice.

The biological and the aristocratic trends were thus
blended in Nietzsche's anti-Christian 'beyond good and
evil', dividing the whole of humanity according to a census
in which the categories of strong and weak were identical
with those of noble and ignoble, the first being the morality
of born masters, and the second of born slaves. Like Plato
in the *Gorgias*, he then proceeded to point out the difference
between these two sets of morality. And, once again, he
saw the true test of a master's rightful power and nobility
in a superabundance of vitality, combined with the
capacity for being creatively hard – first of all with himself

and then with his equals. As for the others, the 'many-too-many', he was quite willing in the end to grant them their crutches and illusions, since after all nothing is more ruinous than a way of life which one is neither mature enough nor strong enough to bear. It was Nietzsche's hardness towards himself that made him repudiate the Christian 'love for one's neighbour', at the bottom of which he could see nothing except disguised selfishness and fear of suffering. The only love that appealed to him was the love for the 'farthest one' – the man of the future, the superman.

'Ye flee unto your neighbour from yourselvs,' says Zarathustra, 'and would fain make a virtue thereof: but I fathom your unselfishness.

'Higher than love for your neighbour is love for the farthest, the future ones. . . .

'Let the future and the farthest be the motive of thy today; and in thy friend shalt thou love the superman as thy motive.

'My brethren, I advise you not to neighbour-love – I advise you to the farthest love!'

## 9

Looking upon the present-day man only as raw material for the superman to come, Nietzsche demanded that this material should be treated accordingly. Common humanity meant just so much clay to him, the clay necessary for the fashioning of a new pattern of existence. This conception made him further clamour for those conditions of hardness and perpetual *agon* (rivalry and conflict) which alone – according to him – could foster the best and the highest type of man on earth. From a static life in peace and organized well-being he expected nothing but standard-ized mediocrities. So the more dangers, hardships and conflicts there are to be overcome the greater will be the number of strong exceptional individuals. 'Live dangerously!' was his motto. But here again Nietzsche demanded a parallel development of what he called good and evil features. In his opinion, both good and evil (in

German *boese* as distinct from *schlecht*) may come from strength and be complementary, even necessary to each other. The opposite of good is not what is called evil, but what is bad (*schlecht*). The source of the latter is in weakness, and weakness is likely to be immoral no matter what virtuous and pious garb it may put on in order to camouflage itself.

Ingenious though such definitions may be, one is still at a loss to know how or where one could draw the exact line between 'bad' and 'evil', or even between strength and weakness. Does not weakness often pose as strength, and strength as weakness? It all leads to confusions from which Nietzsche himself was unable to escape. In his enthusiasm for training the superman through a maximum of resistance he was *logically* compelled to postulate an ever-increasing amount of conflict here on earth. But life in terms of perpetual conflict ceases to be life. It becomes hell. Nietzsche even spoke of the *subtilization* of evil, in which he was ready to see a symptom of the highest culture – not unlike certain decadents, who were prone to eulogize sadistic cruelty in the name of refinement. Nor should one forget the fascination which Nietzsche the invalid felt even for the crude and brutal strength of the 'blond beast', as a contrast to his own physical condition. His extreme utterances of this kind make unpleasant reading. They should be read not as a philosophic creed, but as a document of a psychological state. Such a notorious tirade as the one below, taken from *The Will to Power*, can serve as an example of the confusing and dangerous dramatization of his own antipodes.

'Let us halt for a moment', he reasons, 'before this symptom of *highest* culture – I call it the *pessimism of strength*. Man no longer requires a justification of evil; justification is precisely what he abhors; he enjoys evil, *pur, cru*; he regards purposeless evil as the most interesting kind of evil. If he required a God in the past, he now delights in cosmic disorder without a God, a world of accident, to the essence of which belong terror, ambiguity and seductiveness. In a state of this sort, it is precisely *goodness* which requires to be justified – that is to say, it must either have an evil and dangerous basis, or else it must contain a vast amount of stupidity; in which case it still pleases. Animality no longer awakens terror now; a very intellectual and happy wanton spirit in favour of the animal in man is, in such periods, the most triumphant form of spirituality. Man is now strong enough to be able to feel ashamed of his *belief in God*. He may now play the devil's advocate afresh. If in practice he pretends to uphold virtue, it will be for those reasons which lead virtue to be associated with subtlety, cunning, the lust for gain and a form of lust for power.'

The line between the superman and the subman (or the super-beast, if you like) is thus obliterated. And when this happens, the subman is bound to be triumphant. But passages of this kind should not be taken in isolation, that is, out of the context of the whole of Nietzsche's work. For here, too, it was Nietzsche himself who made the necessary corrections.

10

One important correction was his statement that mere power, devoid of an adequately high aspiration, is always in danger of lapsing into brutality. And so once more he stressed the fact that the right to power should be granted only to individuals who are made of the best and noblest material. As a contrast to the above passage, we can therefore quote this portrait of a noble man, depicted in *Beyond Good and Evil*: 'In the foreground there is the feeling of plenitude, of power which seeks to overflow, of the happiness of high tension, the consciousness of a wealth which would fain give and bestow; the noble man also helps the unfortunate, but not – or scarcely – out of pity, but rather from an impulse of superabundance of power.'

Well and good. But the trouble still lies in the vagueness of the words used, all of which are fluid enough to be interpreted in several ways. What exactly does Nietzsche mean by the 'happiness of high tension'? Or by 'plenitude', or even by 'power'? The contents of these words are bound to vary with the plane of consciousness upon which they are taken, and two men can label with one and the same word entirely different things. This does not lessen the possible confusion – least of all in ethics. No wonder that Nietzsche had to rely primarily on man's innate decency and nobility, failing which no 'table of values' would be of any avail, unless it were imposed and controlled by adequate dictatorial or totalitarian methods. 'I deprive you of everything, of God, of duty – now you must stand the severest test of a noble nature. For here the way lies open for the profligate – take care.' Nietzsche – with an essentially noble nature – stood the test. But how could he expect others to do the same unless he idealized man as he is beyond all deserts? If God is irrevocably 'dead', then man alone becomes the measure of all things. And since there is no absolute (and therefore obligatory) common standard of measure, each individual is free to regard himself as the centre of the universe and to see in the caprices of his own self-will the only thing that is right – right for him.

Even in an undoubtedly noble nature the morality of self-will may drift, sooner or later, towards self-glorification and self-aggrandizement. And so it does. According to Nietzsche, the noble type of man, being a determiner of values, does not require to be approved of. 'He passes the judgement: What is injurious to me is injurious in itself; he knows that it is he himself only who confers honour on things; he is a *creator of values*. He honours whatever he recognizes in himself; such morality is self-glorification.'* But this is only one of the conclusions implicit in the moral chaos caused by the 'death' of God. What is more, self-glorification in its extreme form was eventually to mark the climax of Nietzsche's own inner crisis, which could not but end in a catastrophe.

* *Beyond Good and Evil.*

# 6 The last act

While writing and issuing the consecutive parts of his *Thus Spake Zarathustra*, Nietzsche was particularly sensitive to the neglect on the part of the German press and public. The conspiracy of silence which had begun on the publication of his first book, *The Birth of Tragedy*, continued. And when his writings were not ignored, they were savagely attacked – his 'unpatriotic' essay on David Friedrich Strauss, for example. But oppressive though such an attitude must have been, it only sharpened Nietzsche's aggressive temper and at the same time increased his working capacity which was at its height during the last four or five years of his creative life, that is, during the whole of his third period. The real stimulus behind his enormous output at the time was, of course, his belief in the great self-imposed mission which, in his opinion, was bound to affect the future of mankind. While clinging to this powerful psychic expedient, he naturally hoped that his ideas might at last arouse some interest among the Germans, but he hoped in vain. Apart from such good friends as Peter Gast, only very few readers paid attention to what he had to say. Even Erwin Rohde, then professor at Leipzig University, began to treat him condescendingly – almost as one would treat a failure.

One of the reasons why Nietzsche wanted to see more belief in his task and work was his secret lack of self-confidence – a feature which he was always careful to hide from himself and from others. Hence the eagerness with which he clung to those few friends who believed in him, whom he could trust, and whose talents he often exaggerated in order to make them appear more significant. And how much he prized that loving solicitude which he always needed but rarely obtained! As early as 1874 he wrote to Erwin Rohde: 'To tell the truth, I live through you; I advance by leaning upon your shoulder, for my self-

esteem is wretchedly weak, and you have to assure me of
my own worth again and again.' To the same correspondent
he admitted in March 1881: 'Friends like you help me to
sustain my belief in myself.' And on 20 August 1880 he
confessed in a letter to Peter Gast that 'even now the whole
of my philosophy totters after one hour's sympathetic
intercourse with total strangers! It seems to me so foolish
to insist on being in the right at the expense of love, and
*not to impart one's best* for fear of destroying sympathy.
*Hinc meae lacrimae.'\**

But in his case love of this kind was not the usual experience. Always inclined to idealize his friends, he was the
more disappointed on losing them. This only made his
isolation a greater burden. What he felt about it can be
gathered from these lines addressed to his sister on 8 July
1886: 'Like a stranger and an outcast I move among them
– not one of their words or looks reaches me any longer.
I am dumb – for no one understands me! . . . It is terrible
to be condemned to silence when one has so much to say.'
Even greater despair is recorded in these two sentences,
taken from a draft for his *Will to Power*: 'It has now lasted
ten years: no more sound penetrates to me – a land
without rain. A man must have a vast amount of humanity
at his disposal in order not to pine away in such a drought.'

**2**

Nietzsche's only means of temporarily forgetting that
'drought' was to transmute it in such a manner as to be
able to see in it the price he *had* to pay for his exceptional
mission, as well as for his own assumed superiority over
the rest of mankind. Is it then surprising that he made a
virtue out of necessity and looked upon his isolation as a
privilege of which he could feel truly proud? Having
hypnotized himself into the belief that his loneliness was
bound to be commensurate with the importance of his
great but premature life-work, he was free to interpret his
predicament not as something that had been forced upon
him, but as a voluntarily accepted or even welcomed

\* Hence my tears.

privilege of a great and exceptional nature. It was not the world that rejected him; it was he himself who rejected such a world with its 'gilded and falsified populace'. Hence his assertion in *Beyond Good and Evil* that 'he shall be the greatest who can be the most solitary'. And even more explicitly in a letter to Malwida von Meysenbug (on 12 May 1887): 'There is no longer an alternative. That which bids me live, my exceptional and enormous task, also bids me keep out of the way of men so that I should not attach myself to anyone.' This, incidentally, was also one of the psychological sources of Nietzsche's 'pathos of distance'. But the doubt remained. Feeling at times sceptical of his 'exceptional and enormous task', he resented any sign of uncertainty about it on the part of others. So his isolation, too, became a kind of self-defence, erected against those people whose prying scepticism was likely to diminish his much-needed faith in himself.

His correspondence is full of indications to this effect. 'One must keep out of the way of the kind of creature who does not understand awe and respect,' he said, when referring to Lou in one of his letters to Malwida. In another letter (August 1883) he warned his sister in unambiguous terms: 'Remember, my dear sister, never to remind me either by word of mouth or in writing of those matters which might deprive me of confidence in myself, aye, of the very pivot of my existence hitherto.' And about a year earlier (July 1882) he confessed to Erwin Rohde that his own manner of visualizing things on a large scale was, in essence, romantic self-defence. He also stressed the fact that without a goal which he could regard as important beyond words he would not have survived the trials he had had to endure. 'This is really my only excuse for the kind of literature I have been producing ever since 1875; it is my recipe, my self-concocted medicine against disgust with life.' Since his illness, isolation and helplessness kept steadily increasing, he found it necessary to increase the doses of his 'self-concocted medicine' according to the needs of the moment, or of the situation. What at first may have been with him but wishful thinking became, step by step, a necessary compensation which he embraced the more tenaciously the more he suspected what its loss would mean to him. 'You do not even seem to be remotely conscious', he reproached his sister in a letter (1888) 'of the fact that you are the next of kin to a man whose destiny is to decide the fate of millennia – speaking quite literally, I hold the future of mankind in my hand. . . . The task that has fallen upon me is after all due to my own nature – and in this manner alone have I now some idea of the happiness that has been in store for me all this time. I play with a burden which would crush any other mortal. What I have to accomplish is *terrifying* in every sense of the word. I do not challenge individuals – I challenge the world of mankind with a terrific indictment. Whether the judgement falls for or against us, my name will in any case be linked up with a fatality the magnitude of which is unutterable.'

No wonder he resented the indifference on the part of the Germans of whom he complained to his friend Baron von Seydlitz as late as 1888: 'Look at my dear Germans! Although I am in my forty-fifth year, and have published about fifteen books, no one in Germany has yet succeeded in writing even a moderately good review of any of my works.' And on 21 December of the same year he wrote rather bluntly to his mother that the Germans were 'too stupid for the loftiness of my spirit', whereas everywhere else – in St Petersburg, Paris, Stockholm, Vienna and New York – he already had plenty of admirers 'even among the most exceptional and influential people'.

### 3

This, too, was an exaggeration at the time, but a forgivable one. As it happened the first appreciations of his ideas had reached him by then from France and Scandinavia. Hippolyte Taine, to whom Nietzsche had sent a copy of *Beyond Good and Evil* (another book he had to print at his own expense), answered with an enthusiastic letter. The Danish critic and literary historian, Georg Brandes was so impressed by *The Genealogy of Morals* that he gave a course of lectures at Copenhagen University about

Nietzsche's philosophy. In Sweden again August Strindberg was carried away by Nietzsche's views and even
reflected some of them in his own writings: in such a novel
as his *Tchandala*, for instance. Further interest in Nietzsche
was noticeable in Russia where his radical individualism
was soon to be taken up by a number of modernist poets.

Nietzsche's correspondence with Brandes is of particular value: partly on account of its frankness on both sides,
and partly because it continued until the very moment of
Nietzsche's collapse. Needless to say, Brandes proved to
be not only a generous and understanding reader of his
works, but also a benevolent critic, friend and adviser.
Still, even this interest in Nietzsche's writings was not
enough to alleviate the 'drought' of which he so bitterly
complained, while – in the very teeth of indifference –
continuing to insist upon the greatness of his work. After
all, what did it matter if the present generation accepted
him or not? The future was on his side, of this he was sure,
or wanted to be sure. As he said in a letter to Professor
Overbeck already in May 1884: 'If I did not go so far that
for thousands of years people will make their highest vows
in my name, then I have achieved nothing according to my
own judgement.' Two years later he wrote to the philosopher Paul Deussen (his one-time schoolfellow at Pforta):
'Was ever anyone's attitude towards things more daring
than mine? But one must be able to bear it; this is the test;
I am indifferent to what one "says" or "thinks" about it.
After all – I want to be right not for today or tomorrow, but
for the millennia.' And in February 1888 he assured Baron
von Seydlitz in even more categorical terms: 'It is quite possible that I am the first philosopher of our age, yea – perhaps
even something more than that, something fateful and
decisive on the very threshold dividing the two millennia.'

The supposed magnitude of his task thus compensated
him for his doubts of himself, for his loneliness and
frustrations. He finally reached a stage at which he
imagined himself as standing so high above ordinary
mortals that even company or friendship with them would
be a kind of pollution for him. On the self-erected pinnacle,

where he now stood, the distance from other human beings was experienced no longer as pain but as a source of pride and ecstasy over his own exceptional role among men. It was at this stage that he wrote: 'Neither do I believe that I could love anyone, for this would involve the supposition that at last – O wonder of wonders! – I had found a man of my own rank.' But here he fell a prey to another lurking danger – the danger of titanic self-inflation, of megalomania.

### 4

We need not deal with all the phases of this process which evidently kept increasing while his nerves and his health in general, threatened by progressive paralysis, grew more and more deplorable. During the very last phase of his creative life there were only three places where he could live and work: Sils Maria in the summer, and Nice and Turin for the rest of the year. Even there he had to make use of all sorts of questionable drugs and stimulants. In particular, the mysterious Javanese drug to which he was addicted in order to alleviate his pain and sleeplessness only made his physical and mental condition much worse.

The state of euphoria in which he unexpectedly found himself for several weeks before his breakdown was accompanied by that kind of emphatic megalomania which often is a sympton or at least a herald of creeping paralysis. While referring (in *Ecce Homo*) to his *Thus Spake Zarathustra*, for instance, he says that 'compared with it everything that other men have done seems poor and limited'. In a further passage he puts this work above Goethe, Dante and Shakespeare. Eventually he proclaimed himself to be a 'fatality the magnitude of which is unutterable' and even dared to challenge the only rival in world-history whom he still considered important enough as an enemy, namely Christ. His two books *The Anti-Christ* and *Ecce Homo* are violent attacks not only on Christianity, the 'one great curse of mankind', but – implicitly – on Christ and Christ's place in history. What Nietzsche now aimed at was to achieve as great a revolution in the history of mankind as the one achieved by Christ, but in the opposite direction. In a letter to August Strindberg (on 7 December 1888) he actually boasted that he was now strong enough to 'cleave the history of mankind in two'. He was to be a new saviour, wrenching both history and humanity out of the grip of Christ. A role less grand than that would no longer be good enough for him, and he said this openly in another letter to Brandes in November 1888, when defining his own *Ecce Homo* as a 'merciless attack against the crucified, ending with blows and thunder directed against everything that is Christian and infected with Christianity; it is simply overwhelming. Well, I am the first psychologist of Christianity, and as an old artillery man, I can turn on it my heavy guns, the existence of which has not even been suspected by the enemies of Christianity. All this is a prelude to my *Transvaluation of Values* – a work which now lies ready before me. I swear that in two years' time the whole of our earth will be in convulsions. I am fatality itself!'

The book in question – *Ecce Homo* – is an example of Nietzsche's self-glorification at its most dangerous. The title of this work is taken from the Gospel. As in *The Anti-Christ* Nietzsche here exalts the reversal of everything the Gospel stands for. At the same time he revels in his own imaginary grandeur, 'Why I am so Clever'; 'Why I am so Wise'; 'Why I Write such Excellent Books' – these are a few chapter-headings indicative of the tone and the spirit of this strange autobiographic work.* But as a reflection of the last stage of that compensatory process which had been forced upon Nietzsche by his malady, by circumstances, as well as by his own split character, *Ecce Homo* represents a highly important and interesting document. The shadow of the superman was the pathologic mega-lomaniac. It was the latter who eventually won the victory – at the price of Nietzsche's complete mental breakdown.

* *The Anti-Christ, Ecce Homo, The Case of Wagner,* and *Nietzsche contra Wagner* were all written between 3 September and 15 December 1888, that is, only a few weeks before his mind finally collapsed. *The Twilight of the Idols,* too, belongs to the second half of the same year.

'This book, the voice of which speaks across the ages, is not only the loftiest book on earth, literally, the book of mountain-air – the whole phenomenon called mankind lies at an incalculable distance beneath it – but it is also the deepest book.' Such is the author's own estimate of his *Ecce Homo*. Yet while seeing all human beings 'at an incalculable distance' beneath his own greatness, he still condescends to become their up-to-date anti-Christian saviour. 'Speaking in all earnestness, no one before me knew the proper way, the way upwards: only after my time can men once more find hope, life-tasks, and roads mapped out that lead to culture – I *am* a joyful harbinger of this culture. On this account alone I am also fatality. Mankind can begin to have fresh hopes only now that I have lived.'

A similar tone can be followed up in Nietzsche's correspondence during the days preceding his insanity. 'I literally have to bear the fate of all mankind', he said in a letter to the editor of the periodical *Kunstwart*. 'In two months I shall be the foremost man on earth', he promised to Professor Overbeck towards the end of 1888. On 31 December of the same year he sent to August Strindberg, who at that time was not quite normal either, this message: 'I have appointed a meeting-day for the monarchs in Rome. I will order the young Kaiser to be shot.' And he signed it – 'Nietzsche Caesar'. He addressed a letter also to the King of Italy in these words: 'To my beloved son Umberto! May peace be with you. I will come to Rome on Tuesday and will see you with his Holiness the Pope.'

## 5

Such was the mental state accompanying Nietzsche's loss of reason due to a stroke of cerebral paralysis. His friend Professor Overbeck hurried to Turin where he found him in a state of hopeless collapse and brought him to Basle. From Basle he was taken to the clinic of Jena and then to Naumburg. Here he was looked after by his mother. On her death in 1896 he had to go to Weimar to be in the care of his widowed sister, Elisabeth Förster-Nietzsche, who had returned from South America.

Nietzsche's insanity lasted just over ten years. He died at Weimar on 25 August 1900 and was buried in the humble churchyard of his birth-place, Röcken in Thüringen. His death coincided however with the very time when interest in his works was awakened suddenly, as if by a miracle, in Germany and all over Europe. At Weimar soon a special institution, Nietzsche Archives, with Elisabeth as its self-appointed director, was established.* Books, essays and articles about him began pouring from the Press, year in, year out. His symbolic superman in particular became a fashionable shibboleth among the highbrows or even more so among the would-be highbrows, with an impact upon fiction and drama in a number of European countries. Authors such as Gerhardt Hauptmann in Germany (in his poetic drama *The Sunken Bell – Die versunkene Glocke*), Carl Spitteler in Switzerland, Gabriele d'Annunzio in Italy, and – in his own way – Bernard Shaw in England have all reflected the influence of Nietzsche's ideas in some of their works.

More equivocal was Nietzsche's impact upon modern political trends and tendencies. This was partly due to his own ambiguity and partly to those German imperialists who wanted to turn him into a politician in their own image. Yet it would be difficult to find a more implacable critic of Germany and the German Reich than Nietzsche was after the Franco-Prussian War in 1870–1. Moreover, while watching with dismay what was going on in his native country, he could not help being alarmed by the rest of Europe as well. It was in Europe as a whole that he witnessed a growing confusion of political and other values heading for that catastrophe which overwhelmed the world less than two decades after his death. This important aspect of Nietzsche's political conjectures, fears and ideas cannot be bypassed. No account of his life and work would be complete without it.

* It existed until 1945, when the victorious Soviet army closed it. After that the manuscripts of the Nietzsche Archives were transferred to the Goethe-Schiller Archives, also at Weimar.

# 7 Nietzsche, Germany and Europe

I

Nietzsche was not much interested in politics *qua* politics. The unscrupulous *canaille politique* in particular struck him as a sign of decadence, and therefore awakened in him nothing but contempt. 'Among people of strange languages did I dwell, with stopped ears: so that the language of their trafficking might remain strange unto me, and their bargaining for power.' When he thought of politics at all, he did so in terms of broader issues, inseparable from his own premonitions about the future of Europe.

This ought to make one doubly careful not to identify certain formulae of the 'popular' versions of Nietzsche's philosophy with the real and essential Nietzsche. Least of all should one identify him with some of those political theories which, not so long ago, used to be cynically peddled by all kinds of 'leaders' and by champions of 'dynamic' politics. What could be more ironical than the fact that the blackout of European culture during the second world war largely took place in his name? Practically all the Fascist and Nazi theories can find some support in Nietzsche's texts, provided one gives them the required twist. So it may not be beside the point to mention some of those Nietzschean tenets which have had a bearing upon the political confusion of our age.

Nietzsche's view that permanent struggle and notably war is one of the desirable disciplinary and 'selective' measures is a case in point. To those who have seen the staggering waste of life through the wholesale slaughter of our strongest, physically strongest, individuals, Nietzsche's opinion that war purifies and elevates the human race sounds ludicrous in the extreme. An age devoid of our present-day techniques might have perhaps found some support for such an attitude: but what possible justification of it could ever be found in an atomic age in which personal strength and courage hardly count at all? The only excuse for Nietzsche was that instead of taking into consideration a future full of limitless technical possibilities (capable of limitless destruction), he preferred to look back to the the great era of the Greeks, or even to the Renaissance. His own view of war was tinted with that superman myth of his whose compensatory nature becomes clear only if we study Nietzsche himself. To invoke Nietzsche as a glorifier of modern militarism as we know it is to say the least unfair.

2

Let us consider for a moment also Nietzsche's attitude towards democracy. We need not refer to his frequent method of thinking in antitheses, in dramatic contrasts and situations. This made him often apply the principle of black and white to his sociological and political schemes, which gave rise to further misunderstandings. Since he was convinced that any elevation of the species Man is possible only through an aristocratic *élite* (an *élite* 'believing in a long scale of gradations of rank and differences of worth among human beings'), he was horrified by the prospect of a future monopolized by the masses, by quantity and mediocrity.

This was more or less what Nietzsche understood by democracy, which he confused with plebeianism. The difference between the two is enormous, yet Nietzsche dismissed the fact that genuine democracy can only be visualized as a universal process of levelling up, whereas the function of plebeianism is just the reverse: a process of universal levelling down to the common denominators. In confusing the two, he saw in democracy, especially in socialism and the working-class movement of our time, a tendency directed against the quality of the exceptional individual and of the cultural *élite*. The masses were – according to him – not ripe for culture but, at most, for general education which, in any case, is primarily a matter of statistics. He also interpreted the democratic and socialist ideas as being a direct offspring of Christianity and therefore doubly objectionable.

Working on these premises, he reduced both democracy and socialism to the rising of the 'botched and bungled' against the superior type of man. Rather sweepingly again, he saw in the modern socialist movement in particular the 'tyranny of the meanest and the most brainless – that is to say, the superficial, the envious, and the mummers, brought to its zenith'. Hence his own social pyramid, with the superman as its apex and a strict order of rank as its basis.* In this totalitarian system he combined certain elements of *Plato's Republic* and *The Laws* with those of the Hindu *Code of Manu* founded on the severest caste-principle. He even hitched to it the tradition of the Prussian Junkers. But while postulating for his *élite* a maximum of physical fitness and power as one of the first requisites, he was obviously in danger of mistaking the means (power) for the end. So it was all the easier for some of his followers to confuse might with right and to substitute one for the other. But here again it was his provocative wording that was often to blame. Some of his passages actually eulogize power in its crudest aspects. In *Beyond Good and Evil* he is even ready, in spite of his cultural preoccupations, to affirm might pure and simple as against right. 'Let us acknowledge without prejudice', he generalizes once more, 'how every higher civilization hitherto has *originated*! Men with a still natural nature, barbarians in every terrible sense of the word, men of prey, still in possession of unbroken strength of will and desire for power, threw themselves upon weaker, more moral, more peaceful races (perhaps trading or cattle-rearing communities), or upon old mellow civilizations in which the final vital force was flickering out in brilliant fireworks of wit and depravity. At the commencement, the noble caste was always the barbarian caste – they were

---

* In Brandes' letter of 17 December 1887 Nietzsche is rebuked by his Danish correspondent because of his violent dismissal of socialism and anarchism. 'There is nothing stupid, for instance, in the anarchy of Prince Kropotkin,' says Brandes.

more *complete* men – which at every point also implies the
same as "more complete beasts".'

Knowing the intimate reasons by virtue of which the
invalid Nietzsche was fascinated by his barbarous opposites,
provided they showed plenty of strength and vitality, we
shall think twice before taking some of his generalizations
of this kind literally. This does not make him, however,
less harmful to those who, for reasons of their own, are
determined to take such utterances at their face value. Why
indeed should not a few modern 'complete beasts' of the
sort try to justify their lust for power and prove – in the
name of Nietzsche – that might, duly supported by
Krupp's guns, is also right? A large body of such faked
supermen may conveniently be expanded into an equally
faked super-nation and thus open the gates to further
distortions. The most tempting of these will obviously be
the setting-up of a standard according to which good is
only what benefits the nation concerned, while everything
that obstructs its appetites is proclaimed evil, and this
meant not in a relative but in an absolute sense – evil in
itself. The cult of violence, mistaken for strength, is thus
triumphantly canonized. Here we reach that point where
a misinterpretation of Nietzsche's will to power is mixed
up with modern power politics in the worst sense.

3

It would be interesting to follow up, at this juncture, the
path of German imperialistic thought from Bismarck to
Hitler and his stooges. One could dwell, of course, on the
part played in this process by the economic competition
between the principal modern nations; or else on the
'inferiority complex' of Germany, so uncomfortably
wedged between Russia, Great Britain and France. Hence
her imperialistic plans and ambitions were more than
ready to make use of that 'adapted' Nietzscheanism
according to which might is the only right. Promoted by
political adventurers to the rank of a 'super-nation', the
Germans were often tempted to look down upon other
nations as their inferiors and treat them as such. The cult

of the 'mailed fist' fostered by the dreams of Teutonic expansion and by the facts of the notorious *Realpolitik* thus led to the two most terrible wars history has ever known.

In this respect at any rate Nietzscheanism proved to be a fatality, but in a sense different from what Nietzsche himself had aimed at. Here, too, as on some other occasions, his scathing criticism of Christianity and democracy had played into the hands of his political would-be followers, not to mention his doctrine of hardness, as well as his readiness to consider a national 'big cause' (whatever this may be) more important than the cause of mankind as a whole. Such a dictum as 'We must learn how to sacrifice *many people* and to take our cause sufficiently seriously not to spare mankind', taken literally and out of its context with the rest of his ideas could do any amount of harm. So we need not wonder that one of the eulogists of Nazism (Richard Oehler) declared that 'Nietzsche's thought is Hitler in action'. What is more, Nietzsche's own aged sister, Frau Elisabeth Förster-Nietzsche, hailed Hitler as the incarnation of the superman her brother had dreamed of. It was under her auspices too that several thoroughly cooked-up pamphlets or 'Nietzsche-Anthologies' to the greater glory of Nazi Germany appeared.

The comical, as well as ironical side in all this is the fact that Nietzsche himself was the last man to have a flattering opinion of the Germans whom the Nazis wanted to install in his name on the pinnacle of world-history.* Even if we take it for granted that in his criticism there was always a certain amount of *odi et amo*, we cannot help placing his utterances about the German nation (especially in *Ecce Homo*) among the severest things ever said about it. He was aware of the bewildering complexity of the Germans whom he sized up in this brief sentence in *Beyond Good and Evil*: 'As a people made up of the most extraordinary mixing and mingling of races, perhaps even with a pre-

---

* Among Nietzsche's posthumous fragments one can find his statement that 'the Teutonic *Deutschland über alles* (Germany above all) is the stupidest slogan ever devised in this world'.

ponderance of the pre-Aryan element, the Germans are more intangible, more ample, more contradictory, more unknown, more incalculable, more surprising, and even more terrifying than other people are to themselves – they escape *definition.*' He also made a number of rancorous criticisms of them which are almost too sweeping to be entirely true.

One of his best-known sayings is that 'every great crime against culture during the last four centuries lies on the conscience of the Germans.' In a letter to Overbeck he refers to the Germans as 'this irresponsible race which has on its own conscience all the great disasters of civilization in all decisive moments in history'. One wonders what he would have said had he lived through the first and second world wars. Already in his *Thoughts out of Season* he defined Germany as the 'flatland of Europe'. He also showed scant respect for her eclecticism or for that encyclopaedic book-keeping in matters of knowledge and culture with which she was so anxious to impress the world. 'The German heaps up around him the forms, colours, products and curiosities of all ages and zones and thereby succeeds in producing that garish newness, as of a country fair, which his scholars then proceed to contemplate and to define as "*Modernism per se*"; and there he remains squatting peacefully in the midst of this conflict of styles.' In *The Twilight of the Idols* he even hurls at his compatriots sentences such as these: 'I despise in them every kind of filthiness of ideas and values. . . . For almost a thousand years they have tangled and confused everything they have laid their hands on.' In *The Case of Wagner* he calls Prussia the 'blackest spot on earth', while in one of his letters to Hippolyte Taine (1888) he bluntly states that all his instincts are 'at war with Germany'. In *Ecce Homo* he even denies – rather unfairly – that the great German musicians were Germans at all. The greatest and most famous of them were, according to him, 'all foreigners, either Slavs, Croats, Italians, Dutchmen – or Jews; or else, like Heinrich Schütz, Bach and Handel, they are Germans of a strong race which is now extinct'.

Among his references to Wagner in the same book he makes the exclamation: 'What is it that I have never forgiven Wagner? The fact that he condescended to the Germans – that he became a German Imperialist. . . . Wherever Germany spreads, she *ruins* culture.' On 10 June 1887 he wrote to Malwida von Meysenbug: 'In present-day Europe I feel related only to the most intellectual among the French and Russians, and in no way whatever to my countrymen who judge all things on the principle of "Germany, Germany above all".' About the same time he stressed emphatically in a letter to Strindberg that 'there is no other culture than that of France'.\*

But the number of quotations is irrelevant. Suffice it to say that even the spurious racial doctrine, subsequently turned by the Nazis into one of their dogmas, was defined by Nietzsche as that 'brazen humbug of racialism'. In a letter to his publisher Fritzsche he furthermore declared that he had always found the Jews more interesting than the Germans. One of his aphorisms in *The Dawn of Day* is a regular paean to the Jews, whom he complimented with words he would never have used about his Germans.†
But how silent were the Nazis about these aspects of Nietzsche's thought! In December 1888 – that is on the eve of his insanity – he wrote to Overbeck: 'I am busy with a memorandum addressed to the Courts of Europe with the object of forming an anti-German league.' One can guess how he would have reacted against Nazi Germany and her ruthless organization of that very nihilism in which he saw one of the most destructive agents in modern history.

The cunning with which the Nazis adjusted Nietzsche to their own political and ideological purposes is, however, best illustrated by the difference between his and the Nazi attitude towards the State. It is known that the Nazi

\* He preferred the 'Mediterranean' music of Bizet to the whole of Wagner. *Carmen* was in fact his favourite opera.

† As for certain negative features in the Jewish race, Nietzsche summed them up in *The Genealogy of Morals* and also in *The Anti-Christ.*

system represented the final phase of that state-worship which had been adopted by Frederick II of Prussia and later received a metaphysical or even mystical lining in Hegel's *Philosophy of History*. The idea of the Prussian State being, according to Hegel, the ultimate embodiment of the self-revealing universal Spirit and, in any case, the supreme goal of history, did eventually sanction – for all its romantic flavour – the brutal 'realism' of Bismarck, Wilhelm II and Hitler. But a police state, in which the individual is reduced to a mere tool piously listening to the decrees of those in power, is bound to lead sooner or later, as it actually did, to the blessings of concentration camps, and the death-factories according to the latest word of science. Yet the truth is that no one has ever condemned state-worship of this kind more passionately than Nietzsche himself. These few sayings from Zarathustra's talk of 'the New Idols' can serve as an example:

'The State is called the coldest of all monsters. And coldly it lieth, and this lie creepeth out of its mouth: "I, the State, am the people."

'It is a lie! Creators were they who created the peoples and hung one belief and one love over them; thus they served life.

'Destroyers are they who lay traps for many, calling them the State: they hang a sword and a hundred desires over them.

'The State is a liar in all tongues of good and evil: whatever it hath it hath stolen.

'False is everything in it; with stolen teeth it biteth, the biting one. False even are its intestines.

'"On earth there is nothing greater than I. God's regulating finger am I," thus the monster howleth. And not only those with long ears and short sight sink upon their knees!

'What I call the State is where all are poison-drinkers, the good and the evil alike. What I call that State is where all lose themselves, the good and the evil alike. What I call the State is where the slow suicide of all is called "life".

'Where the State ceaseth, there beginneth that man who is not superfluous: there beginneth the song of the necessary, the melody that is sung once and cannot be replaced.'

## 4

It is beyond the scope of this book to deal with the influence of Nietzsche's thought – via Sorel, Max Weber, Pareto and Oswald Spengler – on certain more solid aspects of modern social-political trends and theories. His own interest in politics was of course motivated mainly by the quest for such conditions as would be likely to put a stop to our 'nihilism', with its confusion and chaos of values. Yet Nietzsche who, more than anybody else, rejected the State as a monster demanding a continuous 'slow' suicide (that is, a sacrifice of human personality), did not mind postulating suddenly and inconsistently that similar sacrifices should be made to his own idea of a social structure in which the ruling *élite* was to be separated from the 'herd' by an order of rank and what he called the 'pathos of distance'. A scheme of this kind might have fitted into a period of feudalism; but in a highly technical age such as ours it is utterly out of season; the more so because our modern trend tends to raise and spread the general standard of living so as to minimize the gap between the masses and the *élite*. Culturally, too, our problem is no longer how to make an *élite* of the mind thrive at the expense of the masses, but how to make the same *élite* collaborate with the masses on a *level* of culture where commercialized plebeianism would no longer threaten us with its streamlined vulgarity and prostitution of intellect on a universal scale. After all, an *élite* can exist only if creatively supported by the masses; and a high standard of culture can be achieved and maintained only if the two are helping each other instead of being antagonistic and mutually hostile.

Anyhow the choice is no longer between an aristocratic *élite* and the 'herd', as Nietzsche would have it, but between true democracy and plebeian pseudo-democracy.

In confusing the two, Nietzsche would not contemplate
the possibility of a *qualitative* democratic culture, access-
ible to all who are willing to acquire it. Thinking in terms
of rank and privilege, he was therefore obliged to look
back to the past – to the Renaissance period and ancient
Greece – as if such a past could be of real use to us who
are grappling with entirely different tasks, problems and
conditions. When all is said and done, it would hardly be
wise to take Nietzsche seriously as a practical politician.
Still, he ought to be dissociated from those totalitarians
who claim to have been 'inspired' by him – we know
well enough how such inspirations are being manufactured
nowadays. Moreover, Nietzsche in his best moments
advocated even a cultural integration of that very Europe
which his Nazi admirers were anxious to disintegrate in
order to turn it into a German colony. The simple truth
is that with all his vagaries and inconsistencies, he still
remained a 'good European' – one of the best Germany
had produced during her 'lust-for-power' period.

His very contradictions were often due to the conflict
between his physiological dogma on the one hand, and his
cultural preoccupations on the other. On the physical
plane, for example, Nietzsche the invalid may have
demanded strife and struggle as a generator of power. On
the cultural plane, however, he longed for such an
integration of Europe as could only take place if the political
and economic rivalries of the various European States
were put aside in the name of a broad pan-European
outlook and unity. Thus he saw something symbolic in the
famous encounter between Napoleon and Goethe at Erfurt
in 1808; the future possibilities of a powerful and, at the
same time, truly cultural Europe.

In *Beyond Good and Evil*, moreover, Nietzsche pointed
out what he called an 'immense physiological process' of
the assimilation of Europeans and the slow emergence of
an essentially supra-national and nomadic species of man
whose typical distinction would be his power of adaptation.
'With all the more profound and large-minded men of this
century, the real tendency of the mysterious labour of their

souls was to prepare the way for that new synthesis, and
tentatively to anticipate the European of the future.'

One could prove by further quotations that, in this
respect, Nietzsche was heir to Herder and Goethe in
Germany, and to the best cosmopolitan minds in other
countries. His early career actually coincided with that era
in which European consciousness was still a vital factor
even in Germany. But from 1871 onwards Germany
became more and more infected with the opposite trend
in order to satiate her own political and territorial ambitions
at the expense of her neighbours. Nietzsche sensed the
danger inherent in such a trend, and yet the first and the
second world wars would have surpassed his worst
apprehensions. But if this be so, that kind of 'good
Europeanism' in which he saw the only remedy for a
disintegrating continent acquires an even greater significance now that the resurrection of a true European
consciousness has become a question of life and death. For
let there be no mistake: unless Europe becomes integrated
– that is, united not only from without but also from
within – she is doomed to become eventually a historical
no-man's-land; the more so because the focus of history is
already being shifted away to other parts of our globe. If
Europe is to survive at all as Europe, then her political and
economic unity (if it ever comes) must be preceded by
that inner bond which springs from the awareness of a
common cultural heritage. The alternative is either chaos
or else that kind of imposed totalitarian tyranny (whether
from the right or from the left) which can be even worse
than chaos.

5

As a child of his age Nietzsche grew up right at the centre
of a Europe undergoing a process of rapid industrializa-
tion and commercialization, the consequences of which
could have been foreseen. Unfamiliar with economic
factors but at the same time aware of some of their worst
results, he was all the sharper in his judgements. These
were prompted, among other things, by his own aspira-

tions of a European who was already doubtful of Europe.
It all amounted to his verdict that modern Europe, with
her confusion of values and her '*demi-monde* of intellect'
was a prey to nihilism threatening her with a disaster
without parallel.

But there were certainly moments when he had a
different conception of a European future. And since one
of his short-term aims was a united Europe, he saw his
immediate foe in narrow-minded nationalism: not only
in the nationalism of a Bismarckian Germany, but in that
of any modern nation whether big or small. It was in such
a mood that he exhorted all Europeans to overcome their
nationalistic squabbles. 'A little fresh air, for heaven's
sake! This ridiculous condition of Europe *must not* last
longer. Is there a single idea left at the back of this bovine
nationalism? What possible value can there be in the en-
couragement of such arrogant self-conceit when everything
today points towards greater and more reciprocal interests;
when spiritual interdependence and denationalization,
obvious to all, are paving the way for those mutual
*rapprochements* and fertilizations which constitute the real
value and the sense of our present-day culture!'* In
*Human-all-too-Human* Nietzsche expressed his admiration
even for the medieval Christian Church, as 'an institution
with an absolutely universal aim, involving the whole of
humanity: an aim, moreover, which – presumably –
concerned man's highest interests; in comparison there-
with the aims of the States and nations which modern
history exhibits make a painful impression; they seem
petty, base, material and restricted in extent.'

As far as Nietzsche approved of a country's or a nation's
prestige at all, he was willing to do so only on the ground
of its cultural and not its purely political or purely technical achievements. 'It is the men of culture who determine
the rank of their country, and they are characterized by an
innumerable number of great inward experiences, which
they have digested and can now value justly', he says in
*The Dawn of Day*. But while stressing the need as well as

*The Will to Power.*

the role of truly cultured individuals and nations, he expressed also the wish that such individuals and nations should be co-ordinated with each other. 'How many real individual actions are left undone merely because before performing them we perceive or suspect that they will be misunderstood – those actions, for example, which will have some intrinsic value both in good and evil. The more highly an age or a nation values its individuals, therefore, and the more right and ascendancy we afford them, the more actions of this kind venture to make themselves known – and thus in the long run a lustre of honesty, of genuineness in good and evil, will spread over entire ages and nations, so that they – the Greeks, for example – like certain stars, will continue to shed light for thousands of years after their sinking.'

The word 'evil' in this context stands again for that unavoidable and perhaps necessary antagonism to good without which good itself might (in his opinion) grow static and sterile. The important fact is that while laying due stress on individual achievements, Nietzsche – with all his advocacy of struggle and competition – was yet the last man to relish those political and nationalistic rivalries which threatened to disrupt the very possibility of an integrated Europe. Hence his repeated allegiance to European consciousness in the best and broadest sense. When during his mental breakdown he wrote letters to the crowned heads of European States and invited King Umberto to meet him in Rome, he probably had in his already muddled head the plan of a united supra-national Europe.

## 6

This allegiance links him to other 'good Europeans' of repute, such as Montaigne, who openly acknowledged that he regarded any national kinship as inferior to the human and universal one. But as human and universal kinship can thrive only on a high cultural level, all chauvinistic nationalism is anti-cultural in so far as it tends to become exclusive and breeds intolerance as well as obtuse provincialism. Nietzsche, whose youth and early manhood were spent in the provincial atmosphere then prevalent in Germany, knew full well why he rejected everything 'local', provincial and narrowly national for the sake of a larger and more cultured supra-national existence. His Janus-like nature was nowhere more evident than in the passion with which this champion of individual self-assertion at the same time strove for universalism and for a broad orientation – in defiance of all things 'local', that is complacently nationalistic. 'One must not heed men when they complain of the disappearance of all that is local,' he writes in a posthumously published passage, 'it is precisely through paying this price that man raises himself to the supra-national level and becomes aware of the universal purpose of humanity . . . it is in this manner that he ceases to be a barbarian.'

Devoid of both nationalism and provincialism, Nietzsche the scholar set an example of what a 'good European' should really be like. His cultural interests embraced ancient Greece, the Renaissance, and especially French civilization. He also felt curious affinities with the Slavs towards whom he was drawn instinctively, as it were, and often referred – rather proudly – to his Polish ancestry. While still a senior boy in the boarding-school at Pforta, he gave talks on the Serbian folk-ballads,* but in his later years he manifested a particular interest in the Russians who, in contrast to the more settled Europeans, struck him by their capacity for 'grandiose aims, their generosity of youth, their madly fantastic *élan*, and true will-power'. He anticipated the threatening might of Russia and was even ready to welcome it – largely because he hoped that such a threat would make the other European nations (in sheer self-defence) draw more closely together and thus promote the desirable unity among the countries belonging to the orbit of Western civilization. Last but not least, as a perpetual wanderer, Nietzsche spent most of his mature years in Switzerland, Italy and Southern France – at a

---

* He must have read them in Mrs Talvy's fine German translation, *Volkslieder der Serben* (1835, 1853).

respectable distance from imperial Germany in which he saw the sore spots of Europe and the very negation of what was still left of 'good Europeanism'.

And what about the present-day prospects? Since political prophets have been among the major casualties of the last two wars, it is no use indulging in predictions. All one can say for certain is that if Europe does not work out her own salvation, she can hardly have a real future. This problem has been further complicated by the rise and power of Soviet Russia on the one hand, and the US on the other. Still, Europe's cultural and political renaissance is possible only along the path of 'good Europeanism'. An epoch priding itself on having conquered space and abolished the boundaries between continents surely ought to be able to do away with our interminable nationalistic wrangles and to promote that unity which (in his brighter moods) was advocated by Nietzsche. 'I see over and beyond all these national wars, new "empires", and whatever else lies in the foreground,' he writes in *The Genealogy of Morals*. 'What I am concerned with – for I see it preparing itself slowly and hesitatingly – is a United Europe.' Nietzsche anticipated the advent of the supra-national European man even as a new biological type, resulting from the mixture of races. His advocacy of a united Europe is particularly topical at present when integration has become a question of her very existence. And this concerns no longer Europe alone, but the whole world, whose destruction through nuclear armaments looms as a dire possibility on the political horizon. It is for Europe and indeed the whole world to provide the answer.

# 8 A note on Nietzsche and Dostoyevsky

To link together such contrasting figures as Nietzsche and Dostoyevsky is less strange than it sounds. For one thing, both of them were among the most acute anatomists of our cultural, social and moral *malaise*, the symptoms of which became prominent in the second half of the nineteenth century, and in the century that followed. And secondly, they were in a way complementary through their very differences and final conclusions. It is quite probable that Dostoyevsky, who died in 1881, had never heard even the name of Nietzsche. Nietzsche, on the other hand, not only knew some of Dostoyevsky's principal works, but actually acknowledge that he regarded him as the only psychologist from whom he had anything to learn and who belonged to the 'happiest windfalls' of his life. 'Do you know Dostoyevsky?' he wrote to Peter Gast in 1880. 'No one except Stendhal has satisfied, enchanted me to such an extent. Here you have a psychologist with whom I am in agreement.' In a letter nearly seven years after (7 March 1887) he was particularly enthusiastic about *The House of the Dead* which he proclaimed 'one of the most human books in existence', while expressing once again his admiration for the *Notes from the Underworld*. In his letter to Brandes (on 20 November 1888) Nietzsche refers to Dostoyevsky's works as the most valuable psychological material he knows and says that he is grateful to him, 'however much he may stand in contradiction to my deepest-lying instincts'. He certainly must have been thoroughly familiar with that formidable document of human frustration, *Notes from the Underworld*, in which individual self-assertion (or 'will to power') is proclaimed – long before Nietzsche – the mainspring of our actions, whatever one's mishaps and humiliations. In his *Theory of Individual Psychology*, Alfred Adler – the champion of ego-libido in contrast to Freud's sexual libido – contends that 'anyone who has felt the degree to which Dostoyevsky has recognized the tendency to despotism implanted in the human soul will admit that Dostoyevsky must even today be regarded as our teacher, the great teacher hailed by Nietzsche'.

Nietzsche must have been further familiar with *Crime and Punishment*; the more so because in this novel Dostoyevsky had explored another of Nietzsche's basic themes quite a few years before it was tackled by Nietzsche himself. How far the German philosopher had had a first-hand knowledge of Dostoyevsky's other works, is a matter of conjecture.* The fact remains that most of the vital problems which Dostoyevsky had projected into the characters of his own philosophic novels were explored by Nietzsche later, although his conclusions may have been in the greatest contrast to those of Dostoyevsky. Another feature which both of them shared was the fact that the *Tiefenpsychologie* (depth psychology) in their works was mainly a result of the inner struggle each of them had to wage against the 'complexes', inhibitions and contradictions in his own self-divided consciousness. If Nietzsche was a decadent trying to extirpate the last traces of our Christian religion, Dostoyevsky was a sceptic and a secret unbeliever passionately fighting for a belief in the name of a Christian-religious acceptance of life. And so far as the general character of their thought is concerned, it entitles both of them to a prominent place among pioneers of existentialism, although they represent its two opposite poles.

What mattered, and vitally, to Nietzsche and Dostoyevsky, was the ultimate significance of man in the world and the universe. Does man's existence contain also transcendence, or else is he nothing more than a specimen of the forlornness or *Geworfenheit*† (to use Heidegger's

---

* It is possible that during her friendly intercourse with Nietzsche in 1882, Lou Salomé had initiated him, as she later initiated Rainer Maria Rilke, into certain aspects of Russian literature, including Dostoyevsky.

† Rejection, the state of being cast away.

expression) without any sense or meaning in an equally senseless and meaningless universe? In this case the general nullity of the world and existence makes one realize, sooner or later, the nullity of one's own personal life, however much one tries to force upon it, *à la Sartre*, all sorts of emergency exits or '*engagements*'.

The problem may become crucial for a morally sensitive man, since the ubiquitous presence of suffering, of ineradicable evil, makes such a world utterly unacceptable to an uncompromising conscience. 'If I had the power to destroy the world, I would do so out of protest and indignation; but since I cannot do this, I will show my protest at least by destroying myself.' Such is the reasoning of some of Dostoyevsky's characters, and they mean what they say. Whereas Nietzsche devised his own idea of the superman in order to impose upon life a man-made sense or meaning, to Dostoyevsky's Hippolyte (in *The Idiot*) and Kirillov (in *The Possessed*) this would be but a camouflaged delusion.

2

Dostoyevsky refused to accept existence devoid of transcendence. Hence his efforts to go beyond his own scepticism and become a believer in the true Christian sense. In his passionate wish for religion he had to explore the problem of God from the angle of a believer and an unbeliever on equal terms. Dostoyevsky's own youth had been marked by unbelief and scepticism which kept tormenting him to the end of his life. In his twenties he not only became a follower of the atheist Belinsky, but also joined the revolutionary Petrashevsky circle on account of which he was first sentenced to death and then sent (for eight years) to Siberia. It was in Siberia that he underwent a profound inner change. But even during that process he wrote – in 1854 – to Mme Fonvizina a pathetic letter in which he confessed: 'I am a child of the age, a child of unfaith and scepticism, and probably – indeed I know it – I shall remain so to the end of my life. How dreadfully it has tormented me – and torments me even now – the longing for faith, which is all the stronger for proofs I have against it.'*

This position between an atheistic universal vacuum on the one hand, and the possibility of a religious affirmation of existence on the other, eventually turned Dostoyevsky into an inveterate fighter for that very view of life which Nietzsche kept struggling against. The direction of man's will or self-will became, in both cases, of paramount importance. In his *Notes from the Underworld*, as well as in his previous narrative *The Double*, Dostoyevsky examined this problem from the standpoint of social frustration; but by the middle of the 1860's he broached the same dilemma on the plane of the will to power as such. He did this above all in his *Crime and Punishment*, where he grappled with some of the most paradoxical mazes of the Nietzschean 'beyond good and evil'.

Raskolnikov, the hero of this novel, not only took the 'death of God' for granted, but also divided – years before Nietzsche – mankind into two categories: into an *élite* of masterful men strong enough to be a law unto themselves in a Godless universe, and into the herd of common people whose business it is to be ordered about, to 'believe' and to obey. He himself discarded the old values of good and evil with a clear conscience. But he was not sure whether he was really strong enough to be one of the *élite* and to take his stand 'beyond good and evil' in so far as the old moral values were concerned. In order to prove to himself that he belonged to the category of those to whom 'all things are lawful', he committed a murder (or, as it happened, two murders). According to his *Weltanschauung* this was not and could not be a crime. Yet no sooner had the murder been committed than an unexpected inner reaction set in. It came neither from his conscience nor from his logic (which, anyway, regarded the idea of crime as something man-made and therefore fictitious). What he experienced was the feeling of being drowned in the *néant*, in an endless inner void which cut

* *Letters of M. F. Dostoyevsky*, translated by Colburn Mayne (Chatto & Windus).

him off from all human beings without any hope of finding relief from such cosmic isolation. 'Did I murder the old woman?' he wondered. 'I murdered myself, not her. I murdered myself for ever.' The nightmare became so crushing indeed that in the end it compelled him to surrender to the authorities and to confess his crime, even though logically he was still convinced that crime did not exist at all.

It was this aspect of 'beyond good and evil' in practice that evaded even the perspicacity of Nietzsche himself. Raskolnikov's *inner punishment*, which emanated from what might be called man's transmoral spiritual plane, could not be tackled by Nietzsche for the simple reason that he did not (or did not want to) believe in it. Dostoyevsky, on the other hand, explored Raskolnikov's case for 'all things lawful' as well as Stavrogin's – in the novel *The Possessed* – and Ivan Karamazov's. The spiritually devastated nihilist Stavrogin did not believe in any moral principles. In spite of this he too was inwardly so much impelled to confess his heinous crime (the rape of a little girl who afterwards hanged herself) that he intended to publish a printed self-accusation of it all. He probably would have done so, had he not suddenly wiped himself out – 'like a nasty insect' – through suicide.

Another case is that of Ivan Karamazov. By convincing the flunkey Smerdyakov that 'all things are lawful', he had indirectly induced him to murder the hated old *roué* Fyodor Karamazov. Yet during the court proceedings after the crime the delirious Ivan decided to go to the law-court and give himself up as the actual culprit, even though he knew that no one would believe him. Hence the sardonic jeering of his nightmare devil: 'You are going to perform an act of heroic virtue and you don't believe in virtue, that is what tortures you and makes you vindictive. . . . Why do you want to go on meddling, if your sacrifice is of no use to anyone? Because you don't know yourself why you go! Oh, you'd give a great deal to know yourself why you go. . . . That's the riddle for you.'

### 3

While coping with this riddle, Dostoyevsky probed the ultimate depths of man's consciousness, facing the universal *néant* and nihilism as a result of the 'murder of God'. An obvious warning was Stavrogin in *The Possessed*. But so were the shallow nihilists around him who wanted to become usurpers of power for power's and destruction's sake – 'starting with absolute freedom and ending with absolute tyranny'. Kirillov again, in the same novel, is only another complex case anticipating as it were Nietzsche's 'superman', but from an angle of his own. Like Nietzsche, the crazy Kirillov, who does not believe in any transcendental order of the universe, comes to the conclusion that if there is no God, then man is the only divinity on earth: he becomes man-God. But whereas Nietzsche's Zarathustra experienced in such a position the tragic exaltation of man who had embraced a self-imposed task of the highest order here on earth, Kirillov saw plainly that in a meaningless universe any such tasks are as meaningless as are the universe and man's existence itself. All is delusion and self-delusion. Hence the only way in which Kirillov could assert himself was to commit suicide as a protest against such a universe.

Dostoyevsky made Ivan's devil poke fun even at the theory that our earth may have repeated itself a billion of times, become extinct, broken up, disintegrated, and then – the sun once more, the planets, the earth. . . . All this, 'an endless number of times, and always the same to the smallest detail. Unseemliest tedium the whole of it.' Dostoyevsky, of course, could not know that this would be a parody of Nietzsche's 'ewige Wiederkunft' ('eternal recurrence').

In *The Brothers Karamazov* he anticipated, in another cruel parody, also Nietzsche's system of the human community organized by supermen and based upon a strict order of rank. He did this in Ivan's *Legend of the Grand Inquisitor*. His Grand Inquisitor, like Nietzsche's Zarathustra, is a formidable tragic figure. He, too, is aware of the universal void, yet he is strong enough to face it without

flinching. He is equally aware of the weakness and meanness of human beings whom he thoroughly despises, but
at the same time he is also full of pity for them. Prompted
by scorn and pity, he wants to set up a social order plausible
enough to save them from their inner and outer misery.
This is why he divides humanity into on the one hand an
*élite* of 'supermen' (who can bear the horrid truth about the
*néant* of existence) and on the other the vast herd of ordinary human beings who could not bear such a truth. What
he wants to do is to lower the intelligence of the masses to
that infantile level where no problems arise and where,
in any case, comforting pre-fabricated 'truths' are provided
for the use of all the many-too-many. 'There will be
thousands of millions of happy babes, and a hundred thousand sufferers who have taken upon themselves the curse of
the knowledge of good and evil. . . . But we shall keep the
secret, and for their happiness we shall allure them with the
reward of heaven and eternity. For if there were anything in
the other world, it certainly would not be for such as they.'

Both Nietzsche and Dostoyevsky saw – each in his own
way – the threat of nihilism. They also gave unmistakable
warnings to the whole of their age, but in opposite
directions. Dostoyevsky saw the only possible solution in
those religious-ethical values which he derived from his
own final conception of God and Christ. Nietzsche's anti-
religious and anti-Christian outlook, but for his strict
aristocratic valuations (obligatory for the *élite*), was not
very far removed from that of the Grand Inquisitor.
Having started with the same dilemma, Dostoyevsky and
Nietzsche reached, whatever their points of contact,
diametrically opposite conclusions. The divergence between the two is of further interest in so far as it leads,
socially speaking, to two entirely different conceptions of the
human community, one of mankind as an organism, the
other of mankind as a mere organization.

4

In the first case the association of human beings takes place
above all from within; not a compulsory but a free associa-

tion by means of that kind of sympathy which alone can achieve unity through diversity. This requires however, according to Dostoyevsky, a spiritual or religious-ethical basis without which one cannot speak convincingly of human love and sympathy, and least of all of human brotherhood. Hence he clung all the more to a religious conception of life the more deeply he realized that its actual alternative was *homo homini lupus**, however much this be concealed by all sorts of legal rules and systems.

Nietzsche, however, who arrived at the opposite pole from Dostoyevsky, could think of human society only in terms of a rigorous organization, even of a kind of colossal military community, set up according to a severe order of rank. Regulated from outside, such an order would aim at disciplined uniformity rather than unity, with the fastidious remote supermen on top of it all. Here Nietzsche had indulged in his 'aristocratic radicalism' (a label given to it by Brandes) to the verge of absurdity precisely because of his incredibly low assessment of average human beings. His order of rank postulated unconditional submission of the 'many-too-many' to those few leaders who thought themselves entitled to use power in their own right. In contrast to Dostoyevsky the Christian, Nietzsche regarded himself as the very embodiment of that anti-Christian spirit whose 'transvaluation of all values' was going to change even the course of human history in the direction laid down by him.

In his capacity of a first-rate psychologist Dostoyevsky had no high opinion of the average human specimen either. But although aware of their defects and vices (so scornfully enumerated by the Grand Inquisitor), he yet added to his sincere and strong will to religion an equally strong will to universal sympathy, since outside it he saw but universal tyranny, or else universal chaos and destruction. Believing at least in the hidden spiritual possibilities of man, he did his best to retain this faith in spite of all. Hence he came to the Utopia of mankind as an organism

* Man eats man.

on the plane of God-man (or Christ) – the very antipodes of Nietzsche's man-god.

What Dostoyevsky meant by his final conception of Christianity is shown by the *starets* (elder) Zosima in *The Brothers Karamazov*. Zosima's teaching has nothing to do with any gloomy and ascetic tradition. On the contrary, it is an affirmation of joy and beauty through all-embracing love and sympathy. He would have had nothing to learn from Zarathustra's dictum, 'Bleibt der Erde treu', ('Be faithful to Earth'). For instead of repudiating Earth he fervently accepted it, but on a plane entirely different from that of Nietzsche's Zarathustra. To repeat Zosima's simple words: 'Love all God's creation and every grain of sand in it. Love every leaf, every ray of God's light. If you love everything, you will perceive the divine mystery of things.'

Nietzsche, who had to fight all the time for his own health and life, came to regard strife and struggle as essential for the growth of life in general. Dostoyevsky too demanded a continuous striving, but in the direction of that higher spiritual affirmation of life in which alone he saw a future worthy of human beings. Not long before his death he noted in his private diary that there came a moment when the God-man and the man-god met. Dostoyevsky called that encounter the most critical moment in the consciousness and history of mankind. What he meant was precisely the difference between humanity as an organism on the one hand, and humanity as a mere totalitarian organization (from the left or from the right) on the other. The whole of mankind's future may depend on which of these two possibilities will finally prevail.

# 9 Conclusion

On studying the various phases and facets of Nietzsche the man, thinker and artist, one comes to the obvious conclusion that most of his creative work was a philosophy of human experience in terms of a defence of life, beginning with his own. In this process he had to explore the problem of man's existence down to its fundamentals. Hence Nietzsche is rightly linked with such representatives of existentialist thought as Sören Kierkegaard in Denmark, Martin Heidegger and Karl Jaspers in Germany, and Jean-Paul Sartre in France. But whereas men like Kierkegaard, Jaspers and Gabriel Marcel represent the religious trend of existentialist philosophy, Nietzsche was responsible for that atheist kind of existentialism which repudiates any idea of transcendence in the existence of man and mankind.

This was one reason why Nietzsche found several antagonists among those philosophers who otherwise admired his daring spirit. Karl Jaspers, for example, admitted that philosophizing with Nietzsche meant continually asserting oneself against him ('ein ständiges sich gegen ihn Behaupten'). Yet whether or not one agrees with Nietzsche's world-view as a whole, one must respect his *Tiefenpsychologie* (depth-psychology) and the acumen with which he dissected, or rather vivisected, modern nihilism. He was honest in dealing with the bankruptcy of traditional values in the modern world, those that were bequeathed to us by Christianity and humanism. In the end he saw his own task and destiny as nothing less than a complete reversal or transvaluation of our cultural and social life; a reversal that could only be achieved by basing it upon a new and anti-Christian foundation – with the ideal of the superman as its apex.

We may of course reject the solution offered by Nietzsche, but we can by no means ignore his penetrating diagnosis of the age. Admittedly his subjective method of valuing, probing and reasoning has opened wide the gate to philosophic dilettantes, some of whom have succeeded in distorting his ideas beyond recognition. This, however, makes it all the more imperative to approach his thought and message with discrimination. The seeker with this kind of approach can find in Nietzsche's work, with all its ambiguities, a great stimulus.

# Biographical Notes

| | |
|---|---|
| 1844 | (15 October) Nietzsche was born at Röcken in Saxony, Germany |
| 1849 | His father died after a fall; his mother then settled with her two children at Naumberg on the Saale. |
| 1858 | Entered Pforta boarding school |
| 1864 | Entered Bonn University |
| 1865 | Moved to Leipzig University |
| 1868 | Introduced to Richard Wagner at Leipzig |
| 1869 | Appointed Professor of Classical Philology at Basle University |
| 1870 | Joined the German army in France. Injured |
| 1871 | Convalesced at Lugano |
| 1872 | Published *The Birth of Tragedy*, which was dedicated to Wagner |

1872        Wagner laid the first stone of the Bayreuth
            Theatre in May
            Met Malwida von Meysenbug, a life-long friend
            and patron
1876        The first production of Wagner's 'Nibelungen
            tetralogy' was presented in the new theatre at
            Bayreuth
            Published *Thoughts out of Season* (2 vols.)
1878        Published *Human all too Human*
1881        Published *The Dawn of Day*. (Travelled to
            Genoa in the spring and to Sils Maria during the
            summer)
1882        Stayed in Sicily in the spring; moved to Rome
            where he met Lou Salomé
1882–83     Wrote first part of *Thus Spake Zarathustra*
1883        Published the first part of *Thus Spake
            Zarathustra*
            Stayed for the summer at Sils Maria where
            he wrote the second part of *Thus Spake
            Zarathustra*
1884        Published the second and third parts of *Thus
            Spake Zarathustra*
1885        Published *Beyond Good and Evil*
1887        Published *The Genealogy of Morals*
1888        Stayed in Turin where he wrote *The Case of
            Wagner, The Twilight of the Idols, The Anti-
            Christ, Ecce Homo*
1886–88     Continued work on his notes for the *Will to
            Power* (published posthumously in 1901, 1905).
            His mental and physical ailments increased in
            severity
1889        Lapsed into complete insanity in Turin, was
            taken to Basle, then Jena, then finally was
            moved to his mother's house at Naumburg
1896        His mother died. His widowed sister, Elisabeth
            Förster-Nietzsche, took him to Weimar where
            she nursed him for the remainder of his life
1900        (25 August) Died at Weimar

# Bibliography

SOME GERMAN EDITIONS OF NIETZSCHE'S COLLECTED WORKS AND LETTERS

1. *Grossoktavausgabe*, supervised by Elisabeth Förster-Nietzsche, 15 vols., 1895–1901. Another edition in 19 vols., 1901–1913.
2. *Taschenausgabe*, 11 vols., 1906.
3. *Klassiker-Ausgabe*, 9 vols., 1919.
4. *Musarionausgabe*, 23 vols., 1920–29.
5. *Werke*, ed. by A. Bäumler, 8 vols., 1930–32.
6. *Werke und Briefe* 1–5, 1932–42.
7. *Werke in drei Bünden*, ed. by Schlechta, München 1960.

*Friedrich Nietzsches Gesammelte Briefe*, 5 vols., the last two of which were published by the Insel Verlag (Leipzig) in 1908.
*Nietzsches Briefwechsel mit Franz Overbeck*, ed. by C. A. Bernulli and R. Oehler. Insel Verlag, 1916.
Strecker Karl, *Nietzsche und Strindberg mit ihrem Briefwechsel* (Müller), München 1921.
*Nietzsches Briefe an Peter Gast*. Berlin, 1923.
*Der werdende Nietzsche*, ed. E. Förster-Nietzsche, München 1924.
*Nietzsches Briefe an Mutter und Schwester*. Berlin, 1929.
*Historisch-kritische Gesamtausgabe der Briefe* (discontinued after vol. 4), München 1924.

ENGLISH EDITIONS OF NEITZSCHE'S WORKS AND LETTERS

*The Complete Works of Friedrich Nietzsche*, edited by Dr. Oscar Levy, 18 vols. (T. N. Foulis in Edinburgh, London and New York), 1909–13.
*The Living Thought of Nietzsche*, presented by Heinrich Mann (Longmans, London), 1939.
*The Birth of Tragedy* and *The Genealogy of Morals* translated with an introduction by Francis Golffing (Doubleday Anchor Books), 1956.
*Thus Spake Zarathustra*, tr. by A. Tille, revised by M. M. Bozman (Everyman's), 1957.
*Thus Spoke Zarathustra*, tr. with an introduction by R. J. Hollingdale (Penguin Classics), 1961.
*The Will to Power*, tr. by K. Kaufmann and R. J. Hollingdale (Wiedenfeld Nicolson, London) 1968.
*Twilight of the Idols* and *The Anti-Christ*, tr. by R. J. Hollingdale (Penguin Classics), 1968.
*Selected Letters*, tr. by A. M. Ludovici (Heinemann), 1921.
*The Nietzsche–Wagner Correspondence*, tr. by Caroline V. Kerr (Duckworth), 1921.
*Nietzsche's Unpublished Letters*, tr. by K. F. Leidecker. London, 1960.

A SELECTION OF WORKS ABOUT NIETZSCHE IN ENGLISH

Orage, A. R., *Nietzsche*, Dionysian Spirit of the Age, 1906.
Muegge, M. A., *Friedrich Nietzsche: His Life and Work*, 1908
Ludovici, A. M., *Nietzsche*, 1910.
Förster-Nietzsche, Elisabeth, *The Young Nietzsche*, 1912.
Brandes, Georg, *Friedrich Nietzsche*, 1914.
Förster-Nietzsche, Elisabeth, *The Lonely Nietzsche*, 1915.
Salter, W. M., *Nietzsche the Thinker*, 1917.
Podach Erich, F., *The Madness of Nietzsche* (Putman), 1931.
Knight, A. H., *Some Aspects of the Life and Work of Nietzsche* (Cambridge), 1933.
Mann Heinrich, *The Living Thought of Nietzsche*, 1939.
Barzun Jacques, *Darwin, Marx, Wagner*, including 'Nietzsche contra Wagner' (New York), 1941, 1958.
Copleston, F. C., *Friedrich Nietzsche, Philosopher of Culture*, 1942.
Newman, Ernest, *The Life of Wagner* (Knopf), 1946.
Bentley, Eric R., *The Cult of the Superman*, 1947
Mann, Thomas, *Nietzsche's Philosophy in the Light of Contemporary Events*, 1947.
Knight, George W., *Christ and Nietzsche* (N.Y.), 1948).
Kaufmann, Walter A., *Nietzsche; Philosopher, Psychologist, Antichrist* (Princeton), 1950.
Lea, Frank A., *The Tragic Philosopher*, 1957.
*International Nietzsche Bibliography*, ed. by H. W. Reichert and K. Schlechta (N. Carolina Studies in Comp. Lit) 1960.
Hanna, Thomas, *The Lyrical Existentialists*. On Nietzsche, Kierkegaard and Camus (N.Y.), 1962.
Peters, Heinz F., *My Sister, My Spouse*, Gollancz 1963.
Love, Frederick R., *Young Nietzsche and the Wagnerian Experience* (University of N. Carolina Studies in Germanic Languages and Literature), 1963.
Brinton, Clarence C., *Nietzsche*, 1965.
Clive Geoffrey (ed.), *The Philosophy of Nietzsche* (N.Y.), 1965.
Danto, Arthur C., *Nietzsche as Philosopher*, 1965.
Hollingdale, R. J., *Nietzsche, the Man and his Philosophy*, 1965.
Morgan, George A., *What Nietzsche Means*, 1965.
Heller, Erich, *Nietzsche*, 1968.
Binyon, Rudolf, *Frau Lou, Nietzsche's Wayward Disciple*, 1969.


A SELECTION OF WORKS ABOUT NIETZSCHE IN GERMAN

Andreas-Salomé, Lou, *Friedrich Nietzsche in seinen Werken* (Dresden), 1894.
Foerster-Nietzsche, Elisabeth, *Das Leben F. Nietzsches*, 1895.
Deussen, Paul, *Erinnerungen an F. Nietzsche*, 1901.
Joel, Karl, *Nietzsche und die Romantik* (Jena, Leipzig), 1905
Simmel Georg, *Schopenhauer und Nietzsche*, 1905.
Bernouli, C. A., *Franz Overbeck und F. Nietzsche*, 1908.
Spitteler, C., *Meine Beziehungen zu Nietzsche*, 1908.
Förster-Nietzsche, Elisabeth, *Der junge Nietzsche*, 1912.
Förster-Nietzsche, Elisabeth, *Der einsame Nietzsche*, 1914.

Förster-Nietzsche, Elisabeth, *Wagner und Nietzsche*, 1915.
Binder, P., *Malwida von Meysenbug und F. Nietzsche*, 1917.
Hildebrondt, K., *Gesundheit und Krankheit in Nietzsches Leben und Werk*, 1926.
Klages, L., *Die psychologischen Errungenschaften Nietzsches* (Leipzig), 1926.
Podach, Erich F., *Nietzsches Zusammenbruch* (Heidelberg), 1930.
Brock, Werner, *Nietzsche und die Idee der Kulter* (Bonn), 1930.
Vaihinger, Hans, *Nietzsche als Philosoph* (Berlin), 1930.
Braun, H. W., *Nietzsche und die Frauen* (Leipzig), 1931.
Podach, Erich F., *Gestalten um Nietzsche*, 1932.
Löwith, Karl, *Kierkegaard und Nietzsche* (Frankfurt), 1933.
Jaspers, Karl, *Neitzsche* (Berlin), 1936.
Podach, Erich F., *Der kranke Nietzsche* (Wien), 1937.
Podach, Erich F., *F. Nietzsche and Lou Salomé* (Leipzig), 1938.
Löwith, Karl, *Von Hegel bis Nietzsche*, 1941, 1953.
Mann Thomas, *Nietzsche und das Christentum* (München), 1952.
Blunck, Richard, *Friedrich Nietzsche. Kindheit und Jugend* (Basel), 1953.
Giese, F., *Nietzsche und Goethe*, 1953.
Löwith, Karl, *Nietzsches Philosophie der enrigen Wiederkunft* (Stuttgart), 1956.
Andreas-Salomé, Lou, *Lebensrückblick*, edited by E. Pfeiffer (Zürich, Wiesbaden), 1957.
Schlechta, Karl, *Der Fall Nietzsche* (München), 1959.
Heidegger, Martin, *Neitzsche*, 2 vols. (Pfullingen), 1961.
Podach, Erich F., *Ein Blick in Notizbücher Nietzsches* (Heidelberg), 1961.
Frenzel, Ivo F., *Nietzsche in Selbstzeugnissen und Bilddokumenten* (Rowohlt), 1966.
Puetz, Peter, *Friedrich Nietzsche* (1967).

A SELECTION OF WORKS ABOUT NIETZSCHE IN FRENCH

Lichtenberger, H., *La philosophie de Nietzsche*, 1898.
Gaultier Jûles de, *De Kant à Nietzsche*, 1900.
Gaultier, Jûles de, *Nietzsche et la reforme philosophique*, 1904.
Halévy, D., *Le travail du Zarathoustra*, 1909.
Andler, Charles, *Nietzsche, sa vie et sa pensée*, 6 vols., 1920–31.
Drain, H., *Nietzsche et Gide*, 1932.
Halévy, D., *Nietzsche*, 1945.
Tibon, Gustave, *Nietzsche et le déclin de l'ésprit*, 1948.
Marcel, Gabriel, *De Kierkegaard à Nietzsche et à Heidegger*, 1955.
Garnier, Pierre, *Frédéric Nietzsche* (Poètes d'aujourdhuis), 1957.
Andler, Charles, *Nietzsche, sa vie et sa pensée*, 1958.
Blanquès, C., *Nietzsche devant ses contemporains*, 1959.
Deleuze, Gilles, *Nietzsche et la philosophie*, 1962.
Gaède, Edouard, *Nietzsche et Valéry*, 1962.
Granier, Jean, *Le problème de la vérité dans la philosophie de Nietzsche*, 1966.

# Index

*About the Origins of Moral Sentiments*, Paul Ree, 55
Adler, Alfred, 128
Aeschylus, 15, 17, 18
Andreas, Friedrich Carl, 59
Andreas-Salomé, see Lou Salomé
*Anti-Christ, The*, Nietzsche, 37, 66, 82, 109, 110, 119

Bach, 18, 118
Baumann, Dr, 52
Beethoven, 18
Belinsky, 130
Bergson, 85
*Beyond Good and Evil*, Nietzsche, 48, 82, 102, 106, 115, 117, 122
*Birth of Tragedy, The*, Nietzsche, 15, 20, 28, 70, 95, 104
Bismarck, 116, 120
*Book of Hours*, Rilke, 60
Borgia, Cesare, 86
Brandes, Georg, 38, 107, 108, 115, 135
Brockhaus, Frau, 14
*Brothers Karamazov, The*, 133, 136
Buelow, Hans von, 15, 38
Burckhard, Jakob, 14, 17, 93

*Carmen*, Bizet, 119
*Case of Wagner, The*, Nietzsche, 110, 118
Chamfort, 23
*Code of Manu, The* (Hindu Book of Laws), 115
*Crime and Punishment*, Dostoyevsky 129, 131

D'Annunzio, Gabriele, 112
Dante, 109
Darwin, 27, 81
*David Friedrich Strauss, the Confessor and Writer*, Nietzsche, 20
*Dawn of Day, The*, Nietzsche, 28, 38, 49, 63, 119, 124
Deussen, Paul, 108
*Dionysian Dithyrambs*, Nietzsche, 48
*Doctor Faustus*, Thomas Mann, 31
Dostoyevsky, 24, 32, 73, 77, 128–36
*Double, The*, Dostoyevsky, 131

*Ecce Homo*, Nietzsche, 11, 45, 46, 53, 66, 109–110, 117, 118
Eddington, Sir Arthur, 71
Emerson, 24
Euripides, 19

Fichte, 12
Flaubert, 23
Fonvizina, Mme, 130

Förster, Bernard, 59
Förster-Nietzsche, Elisabeth: see Elisabeth Nietzsche
Freud, Sigmund, 60
Frederick II, 120
*Friedrich Nietzsche in his Works*, Lou Salomé, 59
Fritzsche (Nietzsche's publisher), 119

Gast, Peter (F. Köselitz), 27, 32, 46, 63, 104–5, 128
*Genealogy of Morals*, Nietzsche, 82, 107, 119, 127
Gersdorff, Karl von, 13, 16, 21
Gillot, Hendrik, 30
*Gorgias*, Plato, 99
Goethe, 15, 24, 43, 83, 109, 122, 123
*Grenzbote, Der* (German periodical), 21

Handel, 118
Hauptmann, Gerhard, 112
Hegel, 120
Heidegger, 130
Heine, 42
Heraclitus, 37
Herder, 123
Herzen, Alexander, 19
Hitler, 116, 120
Hölderlin, 24, 43
*House of the Dead, The*, Dostoyevsky, 128
*Human, all-too-Human*, Nietzsche, 23, 24, 28, 38, 51, 124

*In a Struggle for God*, Lou Salomé, 59

Jaspers, Karl, 137
*Joyful Wisdom, The*, Nietzsche, 28, 34, 44, 49, 63, 72, 74, 75, 86, 93, 94
Jung, Carl, 96

Kant, 33, 35
Kierkeguard, 137
Köselitz, F., see Peter Gast
Kropotkin, Prince, 115
Krupp, 116
Kunstwart (German periodical), 111

La Rochefoucauld, 23
*Laws, The*, Plato, 115
*Legend of the Grand Inquisitor, The*, Dostoyevsky, 133, 134
*Letters of Dostoyevsky* (Dr C. Mayne), 131
Levy, Oscar, 9
Liszt, Franz, 15
Luther, 43

*Madness of Nietzsche*, E. P. Podach, 31
Mann, Thomas, 31
Mariani, 71
Marcel, Gabriel, 137
Mazzini, 16
*Memoirs of an Idealist*, M. von Meysenbug, 19
Meysenbug, Malwida von, 19, 25, 29, 45, 51, 56, 106, 119
Möllendorff, Ulrich, Baron von, 20
Montaigne, 23, 125

Napoleon, 122
*Naxos*, Nietzsche, 61
*New Pathways in Science*, Sir A. Eddington, 71
*Nietzsche contra Wagner*, Nietzsche, 22, 110
Nietzche, Elisabeths (later Förster-Nietzsche), 11, 16, 27, 51, 56, 58, 59, 60, 91, 107, 112, 117
*Nietzsche's Illness and Collapse*, Dr Gaston Vorberg, 31
Novalis (German poet), 12
*Notes from the Underworld*, Dostoyevsky, 32, 128, 131

Oehler, Richard, 117
*Old and New Faith, The*, Dr Strauss, 20
Ott, Louise, 54
Overbeck, Franz, 14, 17, 32, 71, 96, 108, 111, 118, 119

Pareto, 121
*Parsifal*, R. Wagner, 21
Pascal, 9, 23, 43
Paul, St, 69
*Philosophy of History*, Hegel, 120
Pindar, 15
Plato, 115
Podach, E. P., 31
*Possessed, The*, Dostoyevsky, 75, 130, 132, 133
*Prayer to Life, A*, Lou Salomé, 57

Ranke, Leopold von, 12
*Republic*, Plato, 115
*Rheingold, Das*, Wagner, 21
*Rheinisches Museum* (German periodical), 13, 14
*Richard Wagner in Bayreuth*, Nietzsche, 21
Rilke, Rainer Maria, 60, 129
Ritschl, Friedrich, Wilhelm, 12, 14, 17
Rohde, Erwin, 12, 15, 17, 46, 54, 57, 63, 71, 93, 104, 106
*Ruth*, Lou Salomé, 59

Salomé, Lou, 29, 30, 50, 54–60, 61, 63, 80, 106, 129

Sartre, Jean-Paul, 130, 137
Schlegel Brothers, The, 12
Schiller, 24
Schopenhauer, 13, 15, 19, 22, 25, 26, 35, 46, 52, 63, 85
*Schopenhauer as Educator*, Nietzsche, 22, 23, 25
Schütz, Heinrich, 118
Seydlitz, Baron von, 32, 107, 108
Shakespeare, 109
Shaw, B, 112
*Siegfried*, R. Wagner, 21
Sophocles, 15, 18
Sorel, 121
Spengler, Oswald, 121
Spinoza, 35
Spitteler, Carl, 9, 12
Stendhal, 24
Strauss, David Friedrich, 20, 104
Strindberg, 108, 110, 111, 119
*Struggle for God, A*, Lou Salomé, 59
*Sunken Bell*, Gerhard Hauptmann, 112

Taine, Hippolyte, 93, 107, 118
Theognis of Megara, 13
*Tchandala*, Strindberg, 108
*Theory of Individual Psychology*, Alfred Adler, 128
*Thoughts out of Season*, Nietzsche, 23, 118
*Thus Spake Zarathustra*, Nietzsche, 25, 29, 41, 51, 52, 61, 75, 80, 82, 84, 91, 104, 109
Trampedach, Mathilde, 54
*Tristan and Isolde*, R. Wagner, 14
*Twilight of the Gods*, R. Wagner, 21
*Twilight of the Idols*, Nietzsche, 82, 118

Umberto, King of Italy, 71, 111, 125
*Use and Abuse of History*, Nietzsche, 22, 25

Valéry, Paul, 68
Voltaire, 23, 24, 43
Vorberg, Dr Gaston, 31

Wagner, Cosima, 15, 17, 46, 53, 54, 61, 71
Wagner, Richard, 15, 17, 18, 19, 21–23, 35, 45, 46, 53, 61, 63, 77, 118
*Walküre, Die*, R. Wagner, 21
Weber, Max, 121
*We Philologists*, Nietzsche, 27
Wilhelm II, 120
*Will to Power, The*, Nietzsche, 47, 82, 89, 95, 97, 98, 101, 105, 124
*World as Will and Idea, The*, Schopenhauer, 13

Zola, 24